Writing Baseball

THE SOUTHERN ILLINOIS UNIVERSITY PRESS SERIES

Owning a Piece of the Minors

Owning a Piece of the Minors

Jerry Klinkowitz

With a Foreword by Mike Veeck

Southern Illinois University Press
Carbondale and Edwardsville

Copyright © 1999 by the Board of Trustees,

Southern Illinois University

All rights reserved

Printed in the United States of America

02 01 00 99   4 3 2 1

Library of Congress Cataloging-in-Publication Data

Klinkowitz, Jerome.

Owning a piece of the minors / Jerry Klinkowitz ;

foreword by Mike Veeck.

p. cm. — (Writing baseball)

1. Klinkowitz, Jerome. 2. Baseball team owners—United States—Biography.

3. Waterloo Diamonds (Baseball team) I. Title. II. Series.

GV865.K56A3   1999

388.7′61796357′092—dc21[b]   98-21616

ISBN 0-8093-2194-7 (cloth : alk. paper)   CIP

The paper used in this publication meets the minimum requirements of American

National Standard for Information Sciences—Permanence of Paper for Printed

Library Materials, ANSI Z39.48-1984. ♾

Writing Baseball Series Editor: Richard Peterson

Contents

Foreword

Mike Veeck

T
HERE is an old adage that says, "You never forget your first
girl, or guy." Or as Steve Goodman, the late Chicago song-
writer, put it so eloquently, "You should have seen the one
that got away." The same is true with your first ball club. It's
an affair that begins with star-crossed love, very little logic, fool-
ish dreams, and unrealistic expectations. Your skepticism is over-
come by the irrepressible joys of childhood. You have become one
of the inner sanctum, one of those select, blessed few who is
allowed to run a baseball team. It is like releasing a horde of
children in FAO Schwarz. You are the steward of your very own
board game, the king of Stratomatic. Like Coover's hero in *The
Universal Baseball Association, Inc., J. Henry Waugh Prop.*, you
become your club. Baseball cards become animate, oral historians
who star in your personal movie. The biographical information on
the back becomes part of a chain that links you eternally with
past and future statistics of the greatest game in the world.

The beauty of *Owning a Piece of the Minors* is that it sup-
ports the hypothesis that life is not a novel. Rather, it is a series
of vignettes, novellas if you will, strung together by the joys and
the anguish, the expectations and the harsh realities, and finally
the bottom of the ninth. You grow bit by bit in the life-sustaining

realization that there is always another game. That's probably your only salvation. The one real question in baseball, as in life, is, How long are you gonna play? Wayne Terwilliger, Lew Burdette, and Eddie Mathews became common threads in the infinite tapestry that is baseball. By virtue of stewardship of the Waterloo Diamonds, Jerry Klinkowitz also joins this weave.

Another wonderful thing about baseball, like memories, is that soon all traces of anger, resentment, and the hurt one experiences from your team leaving, your team losing, and your favorite player striking out with the bases loaded are filtered out, leaving only the constant themes of birth, laughter, joy, hope, death, and then, blessedly, rebirth. Nothing captures the joys of baseball better than Box 28. The gentle descriptions of Lee and the extended family are my favorite part of the book. If ever a narrative captured the feeling of a ball yard filled with people, this is one. Baseball is made up of, and has always had time for, the little dramas that exist behind the lines, the characters that make up the backdrop, and the bit players and hustlers who provide each ball yard with its own personality. Outside the yard, we may have little or no knowledge of where our seat neighbors live, but in the stands, we are believers, best friends, and witnesses to the truth . . . to the resolution that life lacks. During the World Series, the crime rate in the towns that are participating drops to virtually nothing. All of the town's people are drawn together. People who would normally have nothing in common suddenly find themselves bonded together in the heat of battle, so Box 28 becomes a microcosm of all that's right with the world.

Klinkowitz is at his best when he describes his trip out of the televised Cub games and into the beautiful confines of Wrigley Field. Sandberg to Moreland to Klinkowitz. But wait, Klinkowitz is a ghost, an interloper. But isn't that the point? (Bill Veeck planted the ivy at Wrigley Field, but other than that he used to say, "I have no business on the field.") The manicured lawn is reserved for our heroes. We are not worthy. Baseball is infallible. The business of baseball is not infallible. It is subject to the foibles, idiosyncrasies, and bad decisions made by its operators.

Money rears its head, and when that happens, hearts are broken. Clubs like Waterloo, that at one time were institutions, change logos like socks and locales the way their major league brethren would like to be allowed. As the enmity grows between the majors and the minors, we are more tightly bound together. By the game? No. By the mystique? Sadly, no. By greed. It is a perfect system in imperfect hands. A microcosm? I would say so.

What is ultimately foisted upon the author and the reader is the realization that after ninety years of baseball in Waterloo, it's an illusory world. The confines of the ballpark keep out a world that is neither sentimental nor overly compassionate, and the base paths provide drama containing nuances and subtleties and complexities not always of interest to the general public. Indeed, baseball belongs to a legion of followers who share in the wonderful secret about the ebb and flow of the game. It also belongs to a few business people who don't have respect for the game. Baseball, business. Don't confuse the two. Baseball is theatre. Business is proverbial. Runs: we all hope we have a good one. Hits: an occasional brush with greatness. Errors: the human condition.

Mildred is obviously the heroine of this book. She exemplifies all that's good, not just in baseball but in the human condition. She has the strength, the courage, and the willingness to take on Goliath with a single sling and then walks away in stylish fashion. But perhaps the most intriguing aspect of this book is that it cries out for a sequel five years down the road. I believe, and I think you will too when you finish, that there are a few more vignettes to be written, a number of things still to be worked out in the author's mind. And when we find, with passing years, the part of us that remains forever young, the part of us that isn't cynical and that hasn't been hurt by the one who got away, the rough edges will be rounded and, indeed, like a perfect baseball, or a perfect world. This sphere, or the music therein, will be sweeter. Play ball!

Preface

OR seventeen years, from 1978 to 1994, I was involved in owning and operating a minor league baseball team. At the start, it wasn't anything fashionable to do; I only had the chance because the minors were bankrupt and declassé, nobody else much wanting to get involved with such a losing proposition. By the time I got out, such status had risen to the level of being thematics for prime time television commercials.

"Your own minor league baseball team," the slogan went, as a grinning suit-and-tie type was being photographed with his twenty-five bush league players: "one million dollars." Then, over a second photo, a shot of the product advertised, came another line: "Your own Bic shaver: thirty-nine cents." The point of this comparison? "Two great deals."

It *was* a great deal; by 1994 previously worthless franchises were changing hands for as much as three million dollars. Plus baseball in general and the minor leagues in particular were ragingly popular and immensely profitable. Owning such a club was now a double fantasy: having the perfect toy and making a fortune to boot.

The following chapters tell of my minor league involvement seven ways, as for me the experience comprised at least seven different stories. Simply how I got involved, worked at the trade, and then got out again scarcely begins to give a full picture, for my minor league connections gave me access to things like World Series tickets and press passes to big league parks. In addition to these activities at home and away, I was writing fiction about a mythical ball club only slightly crazier than my own, starting with a book of stories called *Short Season* and continuing with a sequel in the form of a novel, *Basepaths*, both of them published by the Johns Hopkins University Press. Along the way, the University of Illinois Press asked me to edit an anthology titled *Writing Baseball*. This writing begat other writing. In New York, a professional writer named Richard Panek read my first baseball book and chose our club for the focus of a volume on the minors he'd contracted to St. Martin's Press, a work eventually published as *Waterloo Diamonds*. So there were three levels of narrative already: my actual experiences, my fiction, and Richard Panek's literary journalism.

But even these examples don't exhaust the subject of my years involved with baseball. There were others in it with me—a dozen or so in the fluid, loosely organized ownership group, all of whom acted more like social club and civic group volunteers, plus those sitting around me in Box 28 who eventually became an extended family. All of these people had their own story and contributions to my own.

What was the essence of those seventeen years in baseball? Was it sitting on the bull pen bench, telling the relievers of a preposterous short story I was trying to publish? Selling season tickets and helping out on busy nights in the beer bar? Anguishing through executive sessions, replete with league officials and nationally prominent lawyers, as we fought to save our club? Or seated among coaches and scouts and major league front office staff at the 1982 World Series, kidding myself that their professionalism and its attendant hassles weren't my own?

The truth of it all is a lot more personal and reaches from the thrill of standing on the grass at Fenway Park to sharing a temporary life with my seatmates at home and watching my own children grow up over a decade and a half, when half of each summer's nights were spent at the ballpark. In the meantime, I surprised myself by turning from a youthful thirty-three-year-old into a sometimes cranky, gray-bearded, fifty-year-old man.

Looking back, there's no simple center to it and, above all, no start-to-finish chronology. Facts as simple as being asked to join the ownership group and later seeing it dissolve are radically different when seen from any of the various perspectives. It becomes a different tale, depending from which point of interest it is told.

There are a hundred stories about being involved with the ball club. These seven are, I think, the best.

Acknowledgments

RICHARD F. Peterson of Southern Illinois University got the bulk of this book under way by sitting down and listening to one of my baseball stories (about all my teams leaving town), then asking me to write it up. "I Would Have Saved Them If I Could" was published in his magazine, *Crab Orchard Review*. "Structuring *Short Season*" appeared in Mary Rohrberger's journal, *Short Story*, while "Diamonds in the Rough" was included in Ben Siegel's University of Delaware Press collection, *Essays in Honor of Melvin Friedman*. I am grateful for their faith in these pieces and for letting them be included in this book and for the advice of Neil Isaacs in completing the project.

Over the years, my university, the University of Northern Iowa, provided several Summer Research Fellowships for my baseball work—prompting my son to boast that his father was being paid to watch games. Out-of-pocket expenses I handled myself, prompting an envious IRS auditor to exclaim, "Hey, you're one of those guys who gets paid for having fun!" As always, the Internal Revenue Service was right.

I Would Have Saved Them If I Could: The Milwaukee Braves, the Waterloo Diamonds, and Everyone Else's Home Team

The day before I left Rome I saw three robbers guillotined. The ceremony—including the *masqued* priests; the half-naked executioners, the bandaged criminals; the black Christ and his banner; the scaffold; the soldiery; the slow procession, and the quick rattle and fall of the axe; the splash of the blood, and the ghastliness of the exposed heads—is altogether more impressive than the vulgar and ungentlemanly dirty "new drop" and dog-like agony of infliction upon the sufferers of the English sentence. Two of these men behaved calmly enough, but the first of the three died with great terror and reluctance. What was very horrible, he would not lie down; then his neck was too large for the aperture, and the priest was obliged to drown his exclamations by still louder exhortations. The head was off before the eye could trace the blow; but from an attempt to draw back the head, notwithstanding it was held forward by the hair, the first head was cut off close to the ears; the other two were taken off more cleanly. It is better than the oriental way, and (I should think) than the axe of our ancestors. The pain seems little, and yet the effect to the spectator, and the preparation to the criminal, is very striking and chilling. The first turned me quite hot and thirsty, and made me shake so that I could hardly hold the opera-glass (I was close, but was determined to see everything, with attention); the second and third (which shows how dreadfully soon things grow indifferent), I am ashamed to say, had no effect on me as a horror, though I would have saved them if I could.

—LEONARD MICHAELS, "Lord Byron's Letter," *I Would Have Saved Them If I Could*

FIRST, some key dates. The Milwaukee Braves were born on March 18, 1953, and died on September 22, 1965, their last home game after a hideous year of court-ordered life support meant to keep major league baseball in Wisconsin. As for minor league baseball in Waterloo, Iowa, it began in 1904 and had its death knell rung on March 12, 1994, when the club's owners opted to sell and let the team be moved out of town. I drew my own first breath on December 24, 1943, historically in the middle of Waterloo's experience with professional baseball but more immediately positioned to have my adolescence coincide with the National League's tenure in Milwaukee, for that was where I lived until leaving for an eventual new home in Iowa just a couple years after the Braves shipped out for Atlanta.

Never underestimate the effect that going big league can have on a nine-year-old. Until then, the most boring part of the TV news for me was a dull five-minute segment called *The Sports Picture*. At age five, six, seven, and eight, the only excitement I could sense from this stretch of broadcasting—coming after *Howdy Doody* and *Hopalong Cassidy* and before evening shows like *Beat the Clock* and *I Led Three Lives*—was the autumnal ritual of a football outfit that to my ears sounded like "the Green Bay Packards" (my grandmother drove a stately 1948 model). But in the early spring after my ninth birthday, *The Sports Picture* livened up, trading its monotony of scores read by a broad-faced man behind a desk to motion pictures of rangy guys in golf shirts sitting around a hotel lobby down in Florida telling the camera how much they liked the idea of coming to play baseball in Milwaukee.

Milwaukee? Even at age nine I knew my town was something of a joke, known for beer and brats and polkas but nothing like the big time cosmopolitan stuff available eighty-six miles away in Chicago. Believe me, I knew all about Chi-town, thanks to the rotor on my folks' TV antenna and my grandmother's handy railroad pass. In an era when Milwaukee seemed as isolated as Alaska, she'd send my uncle down there for donuts from a favorite Loop bakery, and when my time came, the pass was available for school-clothes shopping and Cinerama. Milwaukee was just Schuster's and the occasional 3-D film with those awkward cardboard glasses. Chicago? That was Marshall Field's, three television stations (not just one), four newspapers (instead of two), and a movie house where the roller coaster segment sent you flying right out of your seat.

Back to those rangy guys on *The Sports Picture*. Though I've never reviewed a clip of it or seen a still, I'm sure this media event included Lew Burdette, Del Crandall, and Eddie Mathews—not because they were stars, for they weren't yet, but because all were supposedly familiar to fans from their recent Triple A days, Crandall and Mathews with the Milwaukee Brewers. For the Braves, who in 1953 started Walker Cooper behind the plate, Andy Pafko in right, and still had Max Surkont pitching, Burdette and Crandall and Mathews grew into stardom with the renamed team. True, their baseball cards still showed B's on their cap fronts, but kids like myself could conceive of them only as the Milwaukee Braves and only with Crandall taking Burdette's third strike and sending it around the horn from Mathews to Logan to Dittmer to Adcock before Lew began making the next batter up think he was wetting down another spitter for the whole process to begin again.

Those faces from the newscast were ones my friends and I came to know as well as anyone's out there in the world. Because Milwaukee was such a small world and the fans so hospitable, these players who back on the vile East Coast might have been spending their free days in bars or at the track were turning up at Cub Scout pack meetings (where I met Lew) and at Wisco 99 filling stations as close as 92nd and Beloit Road (Del Crandall) and 76th and Forest Home Avenue (Eddie Mathews). It took a while to get the personalities straight. Within a month of the '53 season's opening, it was only the tougher athletic kids who'd picked specific players to be during noon-hour recess games at school. That's how I learned who Joe Adcock was: from Warren Eulgen's mastery of the all-arms, long-loud-fouls both he and the Braves first baseman could rip off on cue.

To help me get in synch with this playground stuff, my father took me out to a Braves game one night during that maiden season. Eddie Mathews hit a home run. I remember it hooking near foul down the right field line but happily staying fair, and after that I had no trouble figuring out what Tom Sloan meant when he declared himself to be the Braves third baseman and swung for the fences at Valley View School. Scores on *The Sports Picture* now made sense, because the Braves were winning—over real life teams from substantial places like Brooklyn, Philadelphia, Pittsburgh, Cincinnati, St. Louis, and even New York (sometimes) and Chicago (nearly always). Just eight teams, one should note: a small, self-contained universe, of which Milwaukee was now a part. And what a part we played.

Record setting attendance—nothing to it. Fan enthusiasm? Sure, we cheered foul balls. But this was a hick town's first bit of rapture with the really big time, so why not live it up? We bought the players groceries, treated them to new cars—anything to make them feel part of the community. As I became a ten-year-old, then eleven, twelve, and thirteen, the team grew up as well. Second place in 1953 was surely over our heads, but here was a contender at birth. In 1954, '55, and '56 we were always near the top in a first division that included legendary Giants and Dodgers teams. As I pushed toward my teens and became arrogant in my baseball powerfulness, there were cautions to be heeded but which weren't. Heady in our independence, my friends and I, who were attending dozens of games each summer, jeered when the lowly Pirates left a starter in to be shelled for run after run and howled even louder when the Phillies sent out shortstop Granny Hamner for some ninth inning mound duty during a horribly embarrassing blowout. "Don't laugh, boys," an old-timer down in front of us admonished, no doubt frazzled by our adolescent inanities. "Some day the Braves will be in this position." Struggling to stay less than forty games out of first? No way, old geeze.

In 1957—too early, according to the oral histories collected these days from Crandall, Burdette, and poor old hard-drinking Eddie Mathews—the team overachieved itself and won both the pennant and the World Series. In an age of Willie Mays, Duke Snider, and Mickey Mantle, my outfield of Wes Covington, Billy Bruton, and Hank Aaron was superior, for as a team they were the world champions of baseball. But only for a single season. Next year the Yankees won it back after being down to Milwaukee three games to one, and in 1959 we blew the pennant at the very end to the Dodgers, out in a hideous Los Angeles Coliseum that on the vastly expanded *Sports Picture* looked like newsreels of Hitler's 1936 Olympics. After this, the fans turned sour, as instead of getting inevitably better, the Braves now turned inexorably worse. Lovable old Jolly Cholly Grimm was no longer managing and playing banjo in the dugout. Instead, a wise guy named Bobby Bragan worked overtime to turn everyone off. Stately old Lou Perini, the only baseball owner ever to be mistaken for the hood ornament on a 1953 Pontiac, faded away as a new corporate group took over, men who looked good in suits. (That's my only memory of them: five or six suits with a talking head at the microphone.) And all those awful players—one of whom, Bob Uecker, made a comic career out of it.

But the sad truth is that my own and my home town's baseball dream ended even as that 1957 World Series was just getting under way. It had to do with being good sports about welcoming the Yankees to town, showing them how proud we were to be in an annual contest that for the last decade they'd virtually owned. We were the new kids on the block, felt honored to be there, and wanted to roll out a red carpet when they arrived on our turf. We hoped they'd take the cue and let their shortstop, Tony Kubek, a Milwaukeean my own grandfather had helped coach in high school, step out first.

Ten thousand Braves fans massed at the railway station to cheer the Yanks' arrival. But when the New Yorkers heard of the grand midwestern welcome awaiting them, they got off the train at Racine and bussed up the back way. Yankee arrogance? Sure. But were they right about the homely bushers we were in wishing to make such a corny gesture? Possibly so. In any event here, right at the peak of Milwaukee's baseball success, we were getting word that we really weren't so big time after all.

As a teenager, I went to fewer games, and at sixteen, with my own car, I stopped attending altogether. With girlfriends and wheels, there were better things to do. Then came college. Driving to and from Marquette University, I'd pass County Stadium twice a day, sometimes during an afternoon game when for fun I'd tune in Earl Gillespie and wonder if a fly ball being hit could be seen from the expressway. It sounds callous, but with the old excitement gone, a lot of other folks were doing the same thing: not forgetting the Braves but setting up some distance, some sophistication, so that we could never be called bush league again.

Somehow I thought they'd always be there. A few times in the early 1960s I found reason to go out to a game with my uncle or my aunt. But friends had scattered to different schools around the country, while Marquette had its own fierce loyalty to Al McGuire basketball and nothing else. Too many MUers were kids from the East who'd never be caught dead in such a goofy place as Milwaukee County Stadium. Finally, when it became obvious that graduate school and marriage would be taking me away, I decided with my fiancée to recapture some of the baseball past we'd each enjoyed independently as youngsters and attend a bunch of games—only to find out that the team was in its final season and halfway out the door to Atlanta. Not wanting to begin our marriage by attending a series of wakes, we gave it up.

At which point I began to hate baseball. Not just ignore or passively dislike, but detest with a passion that ranked up there with other issues of the day, from the emerging war in Vietnam to the bullheaded resistance to full civil rights and liberties. After grad school in Madison, I got a job at Northern Illinois University, outside Chicago, and spent my first months of the 1969 academic year there scorning any mention of the Cubs. Who cares, I challenged—it's just entertainment, as carefully controlled as anything on the tube except perhaps *The Smothers Brothers* and the way Ernie Kovacs used to be.

I knew there was a 1969 Cubs team only because of all the local ballyhoo, typical of English profs trying to show they're not effete. As for what was really transpiring in baseball, I missed it all, with great pleasure. Those great Oakland teams? Last I'd heard, the franchise was in Kansas City. The Big Red Machine? Not in my world, where contact with home came when there was a Packer game on the network and I could yuck up my Wisconsin background with new friends from elsewhere around the country. That somewhere along the way Milwaukee snagged a team once called the Seattle Pilots and were now the Brewers seemed totally irrelevant, given that the whole notion of allegiance was just something to get away from as I got on with my life; for professional baseball, the concept seemed a ruse at best and at worst a vicious putdown of every naïve sentiment a kid or a hick or a rube could hope to have.

In 1972 we moved to Cedar Falls and the University of Northern Iowa, where baseball was even less of a factor—except for real baseball, which meant teaching our children how to catch and throw in the backyard. On one of those Fourths of July in '73 or '74, we took in a fireworks show over in neighboring Waterloo, and in the rockets' red glare, I could see what looked like a minor league ballpark across the road. That struck home, for on a trip through the South, my aunt had taken my brother and me to a Paducah Chiefs game in Kentucky. That was back in 1955, when my big-time Braves hysteria was still mounting and, at the tender age of eleven, I could be charmed by such apparently quaint practices as having to throw back foul balls and afterwards giving players a ride back to town. But I never thought to go to a Waterloo game or even look for stories in the paper or on TV. Our son was now in Cub Scouts softball, and sometimes I'd umpire. That was enough.

Then in the summer of 1977, I quite suddenly found myself divorced, with custody of an eight-year-old son and a six-year-old daughter. What were we going to do? Feeling like an alien, I called a phone number listed for Waterloo Professional Baseball and asked when they played and where. It was in the old stadium I'd seen during fireworks, and there was indeed a game tonight. So we trooped out, bought tickets and a scorecard, and while Jonathan and Nina ate a junk food dinner, I got the lineups and hoped I could remember how the position numbers went around the infield and which way across the outfield.

By the end of the second inning, it was all back: 6-4-3 for a shortstop-initiated double play and 9 for a flyout to right. Who this team was and in which league got clarified by a page in the score book: Cleveland's Class A (second from the bottom) entry

in the venerable Midwest League, about the same place in baseball's pecking order as the game I'd seen in Paducah twenty-two
years before.

Next night the three of us were back, then again for a pair
of day games over the weekend. Within a week I'd seen enough
baseball that I could follow the team, distinguishing the power
hitting catcher (Tim Glass) and the Rocky Colavito-style outfielder (Angelo LoGrande) and getting a sense of where in this
league the tough competition was (Cedar Rapids, with a Reds
team to be hated as much as the parent club had been in Milwaukee). What was in actual fact "bush league" didn't bother me at
all, and for the kids it was nicely to their scale: a small park where
they could wander safely and not get lost, friendly regulars who
in a few weeks became almost an extended family, plus great tast-
ing if questionably nutritious food. Overall it had the essential
smells, flavors, and feelings of Milwaukee County Stadium in the
1950s, if not the hype or the size. Better that it didn't. Keep it
small, keep it quiet, keep it a little bit funky and basically cheap.
Maybe then it wouldn't go away.

As I soon learned, there was no chance this particular kind
of baseball might leave, because nobody was particularly covetous
of it. Since 1904 one minor league organization or another had
made Waterloo its home, most famously the White Sox in the
decade following World War II. Luis Aparicio had played minor
league ball in this park when it was relatively new, and then a
decade and a half later Carlton Fisk broke into pro ball right behind this plate when Boston had the affiliation. In the early seventies the Royals were here, and now it was the Indians. Major
league farm directors were always shifting things around, but the
franchises themselves remained tediously stable, never lacking
a team—just like those perennial baseball figures who never go
without a managerial or coaching job one place or other.

Who owned these franchises? Just about anyone who didn't
mind risking a small loss or at best breaking even. Television had
killed the profitability of minor league baseball by the end of the
1950s, and in the 1970s franchises could be had for the assump-

tion of debts. The Waterloo club, once the showpiece of some tonier chamber of commerce types, had devolved into a service organization project kept in line by a volunteer board of directors. With the expertise of a couple dozen factory workers, school teachers, tradespeople, and the odd beautician and drive-in movie fry cook, Waterloo baseball moved along at a comfortable pace. As such, it could accommodate eight hundred to a thousand fans nightly who wanted to see young baseball prospects develop in a professionalized version of how football and basketball players are trained in college. Radical surprises, on field or off, were about as likely as in a garden terrarium.

I learned all this not just from the score book page that listed Waterloo baseball's board but by getting on that board myself. The 1977 season ended just as school was starting, and the kids and I and their new mother had plenty else to do. But come April, I was itchy to get out there again, and from Opening Day onwards, I suffered through some freezing nights in a parka, with quickly cooling coffee, trying to recapture the pleasures of last August. In a few weeks the weather warmed, and the kids joined me for weekend day games. Then when school was out, the three of us began coming in the afternoon to watch batting practice from a hillside just beyond the left field corner. Sometimes the club sent out shaggers for over-the-fence clouts. Most times they didn't, and the kids and I would pick up as many as a dozen or two BP homers to stick in the car before going in the gate at 6 P.M.

By late July I was asked to join the board of directors. Whether because I had a great mind for organized sports or just was out there every night anyway or because I'd amassed well over two hundred usable baseballs, I'll never know. But within a year of paying three dollars to walk in the door, I was an owner of the place—still paying three bucks each game, which we all did in a spirit of egalitarian fellowship with the fans, but now being on the inside of things.

What this meant was selling tickets in the preseason, cleaning up the ballpark a week before Opening Day, working a few innings every other game at the beer bar, sitting there shamefaced with the others when Cleveland farm director Bob Quinn (whose father had general managed the Braves and who had studied with the same profs at Marquette just a few years ahead of me) read the riot act about our broken-down team bus, and riding herd on our single permanent employee, a general manager who was expected to draw enough fans and sell enough beer and hot dogs to cover the annual nine hundred thousand dollars it took to cover our part of the operation. Cleveland supplied the players, we provided a place to play, and that was it. To be a minor league owner you needed just three pieces of paper: a league franchise (for the cost of paltry annual dues), a player development contract with a major league team (which knew there were about as many places to play as there were slots in the farm system to fill), and a stadium lease (which our city like most was willing to provide free if we kept the place up).

For a decade and a half this style of baseball shaped my life. Remarried, I found that my new wife appreciated precious free time when I'd have the kids with me out at the park. Plus they got into the operation themselves, painting the concrete wall that aproned off the field all the way from outfield bleachers to in around the box seats. At age ten, Nina asked if she could vend popcorn, suggesting that she "buy it wholesale" from the concessions stand and hawk it to customers in their seats for a nickel over the regular price. On big nights she'd clear thirty dollars. Both kids gathered discarded beer cans for the five-cent deposit, and by the time he was twelve, Jonathan had saved up enough of this plus paper route money to buy an Apple IIe computer and write stories about the team for the local shopper newspaper. Today, as adults in Chicago and Iowa City, respectively, Nina runs a court reporting business and has a hand in other commercial ventures as well, and Jonathan writes sports and works editorial for the *Press-Citizen*, Gannett's newspaper in town.

Me? I've got my memories of seventeen years of baseball operations. At first, when its own easy momentum carried the minors along, it was all fun, such as on General Motors Acceptance Corporation Night handing our public address announcer a bogus message that read, "Would the owner of a 1982 Olds Cutlass license number ABC 123 please report to the press box; in honor of tonight's event, your car has just been repossessed," and fielding a question from the slugger's wife about what kind of attire she should wear to the All-Star banquet with the answer "A steel belted radial," never missing a beat.

Then it became more serious, as operating costs rose and we had to pay more attention to dollars-and-cents issues to keep out of the hole any deeper than an off-season loan from Cleveland or a raffle could handle. I persisted in attempts to keep things romantic, such as retrieving first-ever home run balls from the shaggers and presenting them to the players, visiting and home team alike. Corny as it seems, the gesture was appreciated. Light-hitting Junior Naboa spent almost two full seasons here before popping one out. Three years later, when I caught the Indians' Triple A team in Des Moines, Junior saw me watching BP from the stands and waved me over to say two things: that in the interim he'd learned English and could thank me and that his mother had been visiting Waterloo from Mexico that week and was proud to have the ball. A few years after that I was watching Cubs baseball on TV, and there was Junior, playing for the Montreal Expos on the season's first visit to Wrigley Field. You guessed it: Harry Caray had a great time calling Junior's first big league home run, the ball was thrown back as is customary with the bleacher bums for enemy homers at Wrigley, and a Cubs outfielder forwarded it to the Expos' dugout—where a happy Junior Naboa no doubt thought I was out there in the crowd that day.

I kept doing things like this, from making sure a little kid sitting with his grandfather got a batting practice ball (which I'd describe equivocally as "one of last night's homers"—well, it could have been) to combing stats books and background reports to give the Waterloo *Courier* reporter something pertinent for his game story ("Attention, media!" I'd announce to a solitary Don Kruse or Jim Sullivan sitting there with his score book and laptop). I raked Diamond Dry into the infield on wet afternoons, pulled beer for an inning or two when the lines got long, and helped spread the tarp afterwards. And I also attended fortnightly meetings year-round, where with growing consternation we wrestled with wobbly balance sheets and increasing pressures from the majors to improve conditions on field and off.

The big change came in the middle and later 1980s. First Cleveland pulled out—supposedly to economize but actually to gear up their better A team in the faster Carolina League. The Padres came to our rescue with players and, as was customary in their system, had us choose our own name, which became the Waterloo Diamonds. Rich with metaphors, the Diamonds not only sparkled on the field but also reflected wealth as well, because even as operating conditions became tougher, minor league baseball franchises were developing some worth. After years of being so far off the beaten track, bush leagues were now getting attention. There were three simple reasons why.

First, baseball overall was quite popular again. After losing some of its appeal in the sixties and early seventies, the sport was now back in vogue. Some say it dates to NBC director Harry Coyle's dramatic shot from the center field camera at Fenway Park, not following the ball but rather holding on batter Carlton Fisk as he gestured his home run fair in that dramatic sixth game of the 1975 World Series. That's certainly a good image, but for me a better one is the television news picture of those helicopters lifting off the U.S. Embassy roof in Saigon, then being pushed into the sea from aircraft carriers off the coast of Vietnam. With this long divisive national nightmare brought to an end, hawks and doves (not to mention Americans in general) wanted to come together again, find something common that predated the disruptive 1960s. Nonviolent, bucolic, history-laden baseball was a good occasion, where radicals could for once be more reactionary than their conservative friends when it came to rule changes like the profitable designated hitter.

So baseball thrived, but on the major league level had in the meantime grown beyond easy reach. Thus reason number two for the minors' new appeal: They were cozier, less distant, and a whole lot cheaper, all in all much like one's baseball memories of the easier 1950s.

But these were the Reagan 1980s, and so reason number three came into play. Money was being made from everything that moved, and—by the new materialistic standards—quite honorably so, not that Waterloo Professional Baseball was raking in the cash. We'd had to get better on the business side just to keep up with expenses, as was true around the Midwest League and elsewhere. But with baseball's renewed popularity and the minors' fresh appeal, a new style of owner entered the game: someone with the bucks to capitalize an operation that as it broke even proved itself a most desirable toy.

Folks like these were slicker than us. True, we'd acquired our franchise for nothing and had labored mightily to keep it essentially worthless, of value only to ourselves and the thousand or so fans who loved it on a daily basis. But these new people bought low and sold high as a way of life, as instinctive as breathing out and breathing in. Thus, given the nature of the times (just look at the stock market), minor league baseball franchises once worth a dollar plus good will began selling for $10,000, then $40,000, $200,000, and soon $1 million, $2 million, and more. Those three pieces of paper—player development contract, league franchise, and stadium lease—didn't mean you could net much money operating a club, just that whatever you happened to have paid for the privilege would in a year or two double or quadruple in resale price. Through no effort of its own, minor league baseball had become a speculative investment well beyond the most irresponsible wildcatter's dreams.

Our board of directors was now down to fourteen, a product of tougher economic times even as the franchise had suddenly become "worth" something. As for the Midwest League in general, once composed entirely of mom-and-pop operations such as our own, it had almost doubled its membership by selling expansion franchises to outsiders, a New York sports psychologist consulting for CBS Television and a sitcom producer from Hollywood among them, all willing to provide additional venues for

expanding farm systems who'd rather grow their own players than
pay exorbitant free-agent prices. League meetings now had a
dairy farmer from Wausau sitting next to someone's corporate
lawyer who'd flown in on a Lear jet, the smell of barnyard manure
mixing with the silky aroma of a Giorgio Armani suit. It wasn't a
comfortable blend. These big money boys, we were assured, were
still a minority—with a two vote edge, mom and pop could quash
their motions any time, meanwhile enjoying a league treasury fat-
tened by their seemingly outrageous purchases.

But what if one of the locally owned clubs sold out to a celebrity who wanted in? No way, we assured ourselves: All along,
we'd never taken a profit, and selling was in fact a poison pill
option as far as we were concerned, for by doing so we'd end our
involvement in the game and quite possibly have our team moved
to another town. And so while expansion franchises were bought
and resold amongst the monied crowd and moved from one new
location to another, we old-timers held tight—until the inevitable
shakeout came.

Major league baseball had divested itself of the minor league
affiliates it owned in the 1950s and early 1960s, when the profitability of such operations had so drastically declined. Now seeing franchises they'd once dumped for nothing changing hands
for millions at a crack, big league executives got interested again.
Not to get a piece of the action, mind you, though they did pro-
pose a small ticket tax as a matter of principle. Instead it was the
old line those with power always use to maintain their control.
"We must uphold standards," they announced, a statement as un-
assailable as mom and apple pie but engineered to drive out the
little folks, those people so unlike themselves as to be forever
threatening their idea of order.

Thus was born the Professional Baseball Agreement of 1991.
By 1994, the majors mandated, minor league clubs who expected
to have farm system players supplied had to conform with a long
list of specifications. Locker rooms must be a certain size and be
equipped with key amenities. Field conditions were to be just so,
fans had to have so many restrooms provided, and—in the oft-

quoted signature piece of this unilaterally imposed deal—each stadium must build an elevator to the press box. Could rickety old Waterloo Municipal Stadium be improved to meet these standards? About as easily as could Fenway Park, which the majors chose to ignore as failing nearly half of the requirements they wished to impose on lowly A ball in places like Waterloo.

In 1992, in the midst of our struggle to solve this dilemma, a professional writer named Richard Panek came out from New York to gather material on the "rediscovered" minors. What he found out during more than half a dozen extended visits was that for Waterloo it was a hopeless cause. His book about us was published by St. Martin's Press (New York) as *Waterloo Diamonds* and has already won enough literary awards to be considered a classic of sorts. Richard's conclusion was that the minors had grown so slickly professional as to leave towns like ours behind. A rust belt city whose population decline to just less than seventy thousand had been one of the nation's worst in the farm-and-factory recession of the 1980s, Waterloo lacked both municipal funds and private resources to successfully repair the old ballpark, much less build the new one that was really needed. Meanwhile, up-and-coming places like Fort Wayne, Indiana, and rebounding towns like Grand Rapids, Michigan, were finding ways to put up ten-million-dollar state-of-the-art stadiums simply with the hopes of attracting a team. "If you build it, he will come," W. P. Kinsella wrote, crafting a new sentiment for baseball as a "field of dreams." *He*, in the Midwest League's case, was a celebrity from out east who bought the lowly, funky Kenosha Twins and moved them down to Indiana, where with great fanfare and nationwide souvenir sales they became the catchily renamed Fort Wayne Wizards. Today, roller bladers in Central Park and along Venice Beach wear their caps and jerseys without having the slightest idea where Fort Wayne is. But back home in Indiana, folks fill the place each night, as happens in the far western suburbs of Chicago, where the old Wausau team plays, and in Michigan, where you'll find displaced franchises from Madison and Waterloo.

Yes, we lost the team in 1994, just three weeks before an

Opening Day meant to celebrate ninety years of professional baseball in our town. We had a new owner lined up who promised to
keep the club in Waterloo at least for the present while stadium
improvement funds could be sought, something we had tried to
do ourselves but failed. But the city would not extend its ballpark
lease unless upwards of half a million dollars were paid as an
indemnity, supposedly for past improvements. Without a lease,
the new owner would have to move immediately. At the last board
meeting I attended, I proposed that we take the money issue off
the table by surrendering our franchise to the league, whose
president might be better able to deal with the city. My motion
failed, getting just one "yes" vote, my own. When my colleagues
decided to sell the team as is, regardless of the consequences,
I sadly resigned, saying I could not be the Walter O'Malley of
Waterloo.

A good line? Well, it all depends. When I quoted myself later
that day to our old general manager Marshall Adesman, now living in North Carolina but a Brooklynite by birth, he cheered.
Then a few days later on the phone to my friend Bob Weide, I
repeated the line and got a puzzled "Why not?" Bob was born and
still lives in Los Angeles.

Though having been proved a busher by baseball once again,
I haven't let this second humiliation turn me away. I can drive
an hour and see Midwest League ball in Cedar Rapids, which
now has a California Angels team and doesn't seem quite so adversarial. The semipro hockey people in Waterloo—actually outside owners from Chicago—put a college summer league team in
the ballpark, where I've been able to see several of my own students play. My daughter took me to one of the last games at old
Comiskey, and my son has helped me see that the new park isn't
completely bad. Plus there's Cubs, Sox, Braves, Mets, plus ESPN
and Fox on cable, all of which I sample dutifully, even that
phonily named "America's team."

I'm not sure if in this era there can be such a thing as a
hometown club. It's all such a blur these days. Are Barry Bonds
and Bobby Bonilla essentially Pirates or Giants or Mets or Orioles

or what? Carlton Fisk, who played his first pro game here, is so disinfatuated with both the Red Sox and the White Sox that he doesn't want to be seen wearing either club's hat on his future Hall of Fame plaque. Maybe I should send him a Waterloo White Hawks cap, as our team was called back then.

And what of my own motives for getting involved with professional baseball? At age nine it was because of what I saw on TV and so that I could know what Warren Eulgen meant when he stepped up to the plate and declared himself Joe Adcock. Who could I be? I needed a name—and quickly. Then, a quarter century later, I no sooner got involved in operating a team than I began having aesthetic fun with it out at the park and writing fiction about it at home.

The Braves are gone—gone from Milwaukee, but gone from Boston, too, something I didn't contemplate in 1953 or 1965. Farewell to the Waterloo Diamonds, though my un-Walter O'Malley-like gesture lives on, together with some richer characterizations in Richard Panek's book. I would have saved them if I could. But how much of my unwriterly self, the self that doesn't need to empathize fictively with larger than life figures, was lost in the process?

Structuring *Short Season*

I should have known not to call it a novel. It didn't start, continue, or conclude that way, either in its process of composition or form of narration when done. Several times before, my writing of it had taken turns toward the short story form, but never as an aesthetic solution. Someone would ask to see part of the manuscript, I'd make some excerpts, and the response would almost always be the question, "Is this part of a novel?" What could I say but "Yes" and then turn back to wrestling with these materials that didn't want to take any generic form in particular, but which in essence were reflecting the nature of those minor league baseball seasons I'd come to love.

As a kid I'd loved baseball—watching it, playing it, and charting the fortunes of the major league team that moved to my home, Milwaukee, in 1953. Then, when that same team left for Atlanta following the 1965 season, I began a long stretch of hating baseball only as a spurned lover can. Don't ask me anything about how the 1969 Cubs had their hearts broken by the Mets, about those championships won by Oakland in the early 1970s, or Cincinnati's Big Red Machine that dominated the next several years. I didn't know and didn't care, despising the sport for its crass commercialism that hid beneath the cloak of idealism and play. Maybe the Braves leaving Milwaukee signaled the end of my youth. Certainly it marked the end of my naïveté.

As marriage, graduate school, and my first teaching jobs followed, baseball racked up better than a decade of its history without me as a witness. From time to time on Fourth of July holidays, when we'd take the kids to fireworks in nearby Waterloo, Iowa, I'd notice the darkened stands of a minor league stadium looming near the park's edge and would think that I should probably come over for a home game sometime, if only for the children's sake. But for all those years I never did.

Until late in the 1977 season, that is. Then the urge finally hit: Why not take in a ball game? I phoned the park and learned there was a game that night. Venturing out unsurely, I surprised myself by feeling at home immediately. There was the game, of course, but also the comforting and fascinating ambience of the stadium and its crowd. The sights were lovely, especially of the playing field itself, carved out of the surrounding cityscape and preened into an idyllic rendition of the countryside, all green grass and neatly raked dirt. Even just a few rows up in the stands one felt positioned above a wonderful stage, and as the lights came on and took effect, the spell was cast. Then there were the sounds, from the bat's crack and the crowd's roar to the ever-present mingle of a thousand or more neighbors convening in the joy of a warm summer night outside. And there were the smells, my sharpest memories from Milwaukee County Stadium and occasional trips down to the older and even more colorful Comiskey Park in Chicago: of mustard on broiled hotdogs, of hot butter on popcorn, of beer, and of a wisp of cigar smoke drifting back from an old-timer in the box below. Richard Kostelanetz has produced an hour-long tape capturing the unique sounds of baseball, but even beyond this, there is a unique ecosystem of factors, all of which massage the senses and seem crucial requirements for the game to happen. I felt that way in the early 1950s and feel the same now, that folks go out to the ballpark for all of this and not just to watch the game itself.

Like any ecosystem, to really know it you have to live in it.

Because there are so many baseball games in a season—162 for the majors and 140 in the minors—you can't have a sense of what's going on by seeing just a game or two. The system is one of rhythms, and to catch them it's best to see, if not every game, at least several in a row, and to make sure those series are distributed throughout the minor league season stretching from mid-April to the end of August, which in nature's ecosystem can mean up to half a dozen worlds. Here at the start of the season's last month I was catching just a few of them, from Sunday afternoon games in the blazing sun to evening contests in the stale heat and murky humidity of Iowa's late summer steam bath, with the rare pleasure of a night or two so crystal clear and refreshingly cool that one could wish it to last forever. But it was still enough to form a continuity of action with rhythms of both similarity and change—a narrative, in other words. Everyone loves a story, and by going to the ball games I was making myself not just a reader but a character as well, for the ritual of American baseball is an eminently interactive text.

Next summer I was there Opening Day and, by myself and often with my son and daughter (ages nine and seven at the time), saw about fifty of the seventy home games that season. The park's attraction was such that I'd sometimes come early to watch batting practice and then even earlier for special drills. By mid-summer I'd often be out there as early as two in the afternoon, roaming the grounds out beyond the fence to shag unrecovered balls that made it out during practice. By summer's end I'd collected over two hundred. Meanwhile my presence had become so familiar that I was invited to join the club's directorship, a group of locals ranging from high school coaches and barbers to line workers at the John Deere factory, all of whom volunteered their time to keep minor league baseball in Waterloo. When I said I'd snagged all those baseballs and was wondering to whom I could turn them in, my membership approval was secured, as practice balls were one of the club's major assets.

And so by summer of 1979 I was set up with three season tickets and a backstage role as well, involved in everything from helping out at the beer bar to negotiating with the Cleveland Indians about renewing our affiliation as their Class A minor league farm team. The business structure was a simple one: In minor league ball the majors supply and control everything that happens on field while the local ownership or directorship handles everything off field, from running the stadium to bussing the team around the league, which in our case covered large parts of Wisconsin, Illinois, and Indiana, as well as Iowa. Yet even though the farm director and general manager in Cleveland called the shots with the team, there was plenty of local involvement with the players, both in personal and professional matters. As a director, I now had access not just to the business office but to the locker rooms, dugouts, and that most magical of realms just before games when the fans start filtering in—the grass around the batting cage as the players take their swings and the sportswriters kibitz with coaches and the manager.

But the effect of getting inside baseball was less than its effect of getting inside me. In *Ball Four*, one of the funniest and also most sensitive accounts of a player's career, former pitcher Jim Bouton concludes that you begin thinking that you've got a grip on the ball and end realizing that it's the ball that has a grip on you. My own involvement as a fan and director was turning out this same way. Each night I carried the action and ambience home with me, and next morning it was still there—not in the sense that I was still at the ballpark or wanted to run back out there but as a subtle rhythm to my own thoughts and feelings here at home. About this same time in my life, I'd been doing something else special—spending a lot of time in Paris during the early spring, late fall, and sometimes during Christmas too (when there was no baseball, of course). There was a style and mode to this world as well, and between trips I'd find myself reliving my weeks in those quiet little neighborhood hotels and corner cafés by reading Hemingway's accounts of his similar experiences and writing a few such pieces myself. By midsummer of 1979, baseball was working a similar fascination, and so to indulge in it I began writing a fictive account of an imaginary minor league team—their stadium, and their fans—that could make my morning hours as happy and rewarding as those afternoons and evenings I'd spent in real life out at the ballpark.

Short Season didn't begin as a novel or a short story; it started with just the title itself (which crystalizes the special nature of the minor league game, long enough to fill a sizable portion of the year but not as long as in the majors, which runs well into fall) and a legal pad of ballpoint writing. Each day after breakfast I'd take pen and paper with my coffee up to the sundeck. This itself was a liberation, since my literary criticism would have kept me cooped up inside with my books and typewriter. I didn't have any clear idea of where to start, certainly not where the book does in its final form, which is with the pregame activities one night quite early in the season. Instead, I was intrigued by two moments shared out at the real life ball park just a few days before, and not even pertinent to a game.

The first was during some early afternoon workouts. While the pitching staff practiced their moves fielding bunts, four or five of the other players were lounging out on the bull pen bench—a favorite place for staying out of harm's and the manager's way. I spent some time talking about this and that with an outfielder I'd come to know plus did a lot of listening to the others' chatter. One, however—a young shortstop from Panama who seemed pretty shy and didn't seem to have much English—hadn't said a word. Yet he sat with us for half an hour, as comfortable as any of us with all this talk that made less sense conceptually than musically—we were all just killing time and feeling good in the warm sun and fragrance of freshly mown grass. Finally, the Hispanic kid smiled, got up, and moseyed back to the dugout. At once his presence, or lack of it, was noticed, and my outfielder friend called after him, "Nice talking with you, Ed!" For a moment I thought he was being sarcastic, and maybe he was. But it struck me that Eddie had indeed been part of the conversation without saying a word, for he had shared the most important elements of being out there on the bench during this lazy and beautiful afternoon.

The second moment happened a few days later, during the time when the hitters took batting practice, the pitchers shagged their flies in the outfield, and I roamed the fields out beyond the fence with a few kids from the neighborhood, collecting all the BP home runs. One of these kids had been doing quite well, carrying a plastic batting helmet filled with what looked like a dozen balls. We talked about shagging, the team, and favorite players. The kid was eleven or twelve, and it was only after a full hour's BP that it occurred to me that I hadn't taken any notice that this ace shagger, champion of all the neighborhood boys who ran after errant baseballs and turned them in for a quarter each, might in fact be a little girl. If she was, she was sure a tomboy. But she or he was at that age when gender can be uncertain or even ambiguous, and I was taken by the fact that in just a couple years this ambiguity would be resolved. For now, however, her special status reminded me of the Panamanian shortstop's role in that bullpen conversation. Against all the black-and-white distinctions and well-defined roles that characterized the more obvious elements of baseball, here were two richly complex human situations. Both Eddie and the little shagger were out of what would otherwise be their natural elements, yet each fit into the essence of this game; indeed, they might be suggestions of what had given it the depth that had kept me fascinated for so long.

Would they ever come together, to find each other in their mutual quietness, innocence, and uniqueness? I guessed I could bring Jananne, for that was her name, into the game on one of my extra tickets. But there was a much better way to not only introduce them but follow along to see what what would happen: I'd write a meeting into the book and let a friendship between these two unlikely yet so alike characters take its narrative course. That special sense I'd felt on the bullpen bench and again out beyond the wall were the factors I wanted to unite, and I trusted that what I could surmise about Eddie and Jananne would carry the action through.

As a fictive encounter, it worked out well enough, and soon I had not just their meeting but several pages of material surrounding it. That was the truth I was learning about things that happen in a minor league baseball season: There is always a context for everything. If Jananne (who became "Jolene") came in the stadium for a game, she'd be missing her shagger's duties outside, chasing foul balls and the occasional home run shot. If Eddie (who kept his name) got distracted by this young girl, he'd pay for it with his game and among his teammates. For unlike either fiction (where something must be construed) or real life (where nobody knows the future), in baseball there is always something that comes next. Why so? Because the game itself is an already constructed fiction, with a format for action and style of characterization for everyone, from the narrative sequences of innings in a game and games in a series (all adding up to a long, involved season) to the properties that make a big, powerful first baseman (often left-handed as well) instantly distinguishable from a nimble little shortstop (who to make the double play must always throw from the right).

In a few weeks I had about fifty pages, reaching back a bit earlier to sketch in the pregame circumstances and then following as Eddie and his teammates head south for a road trip. The tone and pacing seemed much like a baseball season, what with the relatively level grind of playing day after day after day, but benefited from the flavoring of minor league spice, including all the special things that happen when the players are younger, less polished, and immensely less monied than their senior colleagues in the majors. Most importantly, I knew I was taking the ballpark's ambience and using it to generate a narrative, filling the hours I'd spend out on the deck each morning with the same feeling I'd been experiencing during this summer of baseball.

About this time, my first efforts at *Short Season* found a reader: my colleague Robley Wilson, editor of *The North American Review*. When Rob asks to see something, it's because he wants it; I knew that as an old Red Sox fan, Rob loved the game, and I suspected he saw a place for baseball fiction in the *NAR*. Yet his reading turned up the first of several problems with genre, for the pages came back with Rob's dismay at not being able to tell if they were fiction or reportage. It's the former, I claimed, yet Rob felt the whole approach was journalistic, incorporating as it did so many details of minor league ball.

And so I wrote on, trying to make the bulk of it less documentary. The best way to do that, I guessed, was to add lots of action. I'd heard stories of wild road trips and imagined all the things that could happen with two dozen wild young ballplayers away from home. The result was a relatively self-contained string of about a dozen pages, sequestered and unified by the circumstance of a week-long road trip up north. I'd have the players riding the bus and killing time by making a list of all the little atrocities around the league, from the smelly motel rooms in Davenport to a bothersome mouse that kept them awake every time they roomed in Eau Claire. Sure enough, that night the little rodent starts its mayhem but gets trapped in one of the bathrooms by Jim Smith, the catcher, who attacks it with his bat. Within a paragraph or two, the bathroom is destroyed, of course, and the disruption spreads throughout the motel. Here, I felt, was a bona fide story, one I felt confident enough about to send to *The New Yorker*.

When the return mail brought not my story but an envelope from the magazine's editorial office, I guessed I'd made a sale. But not quite. A fiction editor praised the piece but said Roger Angell had a lock on baseball there, adding that Roger himself had thought Robert Creamer at *Sports Illustrated* would like it. That's where it was now, and I should expect to hear from *SI* in a few days.

Creamer's call came that same day, in fact, bearing the good news that he wished to publish the story. Would I please send "verification"? Verification of what, I asked; didn't he know the piece was pure fiction? Yes, I'd called it that, but knowing my affiliation with the team, Creamer suspected that it was based on fact and that was how he wished to run it—as a true story, a feature article, rather than as fiction. Just send him a letter stating that it had all really happened and I'd be in.

I doubt he believed me when I insisted that no such event

had happened: no trashing of the motel, not even a mouse with a league-wide reputation. His parting words were to the effect that if I changed my mind and was willing to fess up to the truth, he'd run the piece at once.

That wasn't a temptation, but another matter involving borders of genres was. There was a ball game that evening, and I spent much of it out in the left field bleachers next to the bull pen, chatting with our pitchers. They knew I was writing about minor league baseball and were anxious for something to appear in print—preferably about themselves. When they asked how things were going and I told them about *Sports Illustrated*'s wish for a verifiable story, they asked what I'd written. As I ran through the narrative of "Five Bad Hands and the Wild Mouse Folds" I saw their interest and eagerness growing, until at the end one of the spunkier relievers announced that I had no problem; there was a road trip coming up next week, and they'd be glad to do just what I'd described—provided, of course, that I paid for all the damage and covered their fines. For the half second that I thought of agreeing, the boundary between fiction and fact threatened to be crossed. Yet the narrative had worked its spell, for the players were greatly disappointed when I said they couldn't be characters in it.

Fact and fiction tended to blend that summer and during the other summer seasons afterwards. Although much of the narrative was being added in undifferentiated chunks, other parts were distinguishing themselves as short stories, usually because they were centered on not a player or a game but a specific problem. Though I've never taught creative writing, by teaching the short stories of writers who do—such as Grace Paley and Stephen Dixon—I've guessed that some of their own work reflects assignments they might give their classes. For example, write a story that begins with a conventional ending line but that narrative circumstances will disallow from happening (such as in Dixon's "The Signing"). Or, as in the case of Paley's "Samuel," write a story about grief, about a truly terrible loss, such as the accidental death of a child, but try to hold off expressing that grief for as long as possible (in Paley's story the desire to scream, to sob, to be consumed in anguish is withheld until the very last page, when the child's mother is informed and the grief finally breaks forth in a manner that neither time nor space can contain, expanding this very short story to infinite proportions). Perhaps that's why so many creative writing programs are called "writers workshops." My own workshop problem was even more pointedly technical; yet it referred to something pertinently topical in baseball: My friend Richard Kostelanetz suggested that I fill a story with all the things that can happen in the otherwise unmeasured interval between two pitches. Kosti's idea intrigued me, especially because I'd come up with a silly story about seeking the ultimate source of the Mississippi River and finding it a leaky faucet and wanted to work it into the book somewhere. Here was my chance. The early moments of a game, after the first pitch (ball one), would be disrupted by some linguistically based confusion between the pitcher (speaking Dominican Republic Spanish) and the shortstop (who used a Panamanian idiom); this in turn would disrupt a story among the bench jockeys about a trip to the actual Mississippi headwaters, with the result that before the second pitch could be made, at least one player would be confused into thinking that the river sprang from a dripping showerhead (which would be, in fact, the conclusion to an entirely different story whose stream gets crossed during the mix-up on the field). The result was "Ball Two," something that doesn't happen until the story's final line; because my friend Kosti suggested the idea, the pitcher—who's named in the story's first words—is named after him.

By 1983, after five complete summers of baseball, I had about 150 pages of material but no real focus for it. But seeing that my own interest in writing about the subject had been taking the form of sensing problems or projects and writing my way through to their solution or fulfillment gave me an idea for recovering that little narrative about Eddie and the androgynous shagger. Looking back through the pages, I isolated the moments where each of them met their author and where then their author decided to put them together. Extracted, these passages were about half the length of a conventional short story. But these pages told us only half of what we needed to know, a problem I could solve easily. What else was there in the baseball ambience that yielded the same feelings of Eddie and his niña's innocence? For her, already known as a typical American kid, it was all there in the present, especially in her fascination with being taken into the park and down among the stars on the field. For Eddie, though, I had to go back to his childhood in Panama, then take him through the experiences that after amateur ball and tryouts before a scout brought him, confused and frightened, to a North America radically unlike anything he'd sensed before. As "Eddie and the Niña," it went to Rob Wilson at *The North American Review* and appeared there in June, my first published story.

With a story in the *NAR*, things rolled toward completion. The university gave me a summer fellowship to complete the book, during which a summer school teacher covering fourth grade at the campus lab school invited me to read something to her nine- and ten-year-olds. Realizing that the romantic uncertainty and sexual ambiguity of "Eddie and the Niña" would be beyond them and that few youngsters imprisoned in a summer school classroom would have the patience for the intricacies of "Ball Two," I took the days beforehand to write a story to their order. "Rain Date" was timed for a ten-year-old's attention span and paced with plenty of disruptive action, all of which centers around the goofing off by players in the murky delay that precedes a rain-out. It is the little-kid nature of baseball that prompts its professionals to splash around in the water and mud on such occasions, and it was easy to keep the class's attention with my story of one especially colorful player who leads his team in a series of belly-flop slides around the soaking bases and who then takes off on the groundskeeper's tractor to repeat the course. The story's ending, "He's heading toward second on two wheels and everyone knows the best is yet to come," led to several imaginative bids as to what could possibly happen next. It kept the action alive in the listeners' minds and gave them a chance to participate in its authorship. And in terms of the project I'd set for the piece, it kept my character alive, forever goofing off in an eternity of unsuspended action. It made for an infinity of disruption, but also a very simple kind; in the manuscript, I'd find a place for it early, before the more complicated disruptions of the other little narratives.

The *NAR* appearance prompted another response, this time from an agent named Nat Sobel in New York. He wrote me in care of the magazine, saying he liked the piece and suspected it was part of a longer work, a novel. Well, it was, originally, and so I sent him the fifty-page stretch in which Eddie and the shagger had first appeared. Nat replied that he liked the writing and would like to market the novel when completed. And so I set to work producing another 150 pages for a total of 300 that I hoped he could sell as *Short Season*.

Thinking of the book as a novel is surely what brought it to completion, though in the end it turned out to be something else entirely. From the start, I'd had the book's beginning and conclusion in mind: the pregame business that each night replicates the preparations for an entire season and the inning-by-inning action of the championship game that would end the year (these pages were among the first written). Now that I had the motivation for a full book in mind, I began thinking in spatial terms—not so much of the time of an elapsing season but of how different bits and pieces of it, so individual by themselves, contribute to the push-and-pull energy of a summer in the minor leagues. My own sense of the season's rhythm suggested places for the meeting between Eddie and the shagger, the affair with the mouse up north, and the disruptions of "Rain Date" and "Ball Two," all of which I was now calling chapters. From time to time, friends would check in with more suggestions, such as another from Richard Kostelanetz that I do something with the sounds of baseball. Spatially, I wished to complete a picture of the short season's environment, so amidst the action came treatments of the manager preparing for a game, the pitching coach teaching some ancient tricks, a sportswriter concocting metaphors, the public address announcer operating a fantasy life from above, something about the wives, a couple of stories where players would sneak home (or get released), and so forth. One short section dealt with a group of fans; another dealt with the club's general manager handling the business end of things. Once I began arranging the various sections, I gained a feel for the gaps that needed to be filled, and my last summer of work on the book consisted in rounding out the picture.

By September of 1985, *Short Season* was finished and, as a novel, went to Nat Sobel. Friends praised him as a top agent but warned that his strong commercial savvy meant he'd shop the book around to his best contacts for three months, six at the most; if he couldn't find a publisher in that time, he'd let the project go. Sure enough, in three months, Nat had undertaken a massive set of submissions, getting *Short Season* into the offices of the top editors in New York. Each week I'd receive an envelope from Nat's agency holding a rejection letter and Nat's scribbled comment as to whom he was trying next. The rejections didn't surprise or disappoint me; Gordon Lish, Tom Jenks, and Jonathan Galassi's acquisitions are always the industry's best, and it struck me that Nat's ambitions might be a little too high. But continue he did, and as the rejection letters stacked up, I became concerned that they all told the same story: of an editor who admired the writing in *Short Season* but regretted its failure to present a central character whose unified experiences would provide the logical development a novel demanded.

Here was where I took exception. Were this a novel about the major leagues, I could pick such a character, for the game at that level is rich with stars; indeed, the big leagues' spotlight makes such central characterization quite natural. But my book was about the minors, where anonymity is the name of the game. If anyone is good enough to be known or terrible enough to be notorious, up or out he goes. In the majors, a team's players last as long as ten or twenty years; in the minors, you have them for a year or two at most, then they're gone—again, up or out. The season itself is shorter, its attention less focused, and its cast of characters unstable as new players come in from the college draft while others are promoted or released in midsummer. Take the conventional definition of a novel, the one Nat's network of editors was proposing, and a fictional narrative about minor league ball could not, by its own definition, fulfill it.

Yet for more than a year Nat Sobel stuck with the book, compiling an agency record of thirty-five rejections. By the end, *Short Season* had been to every major publisher, in most cases to the top fiction editor there; and every rejection read the same. Fearing Nat would drop the book, I suggested making a change: Given the fact that we could not produce the seamless and developing narrative these folks wanted, but because they so admired the writing and individual sections, why not call it a collection of short stories? Nat never answered, but I knew he was keeping the book out because rejections kept coming in. So I undertook the corrective surgery on my own, retyping the title page as *Short Season and Other Stories*, whiting out the chapter numbers in favor of free standing titles, and packing it off to John Irwin, whose series with the Johns Hopkins University Press had published story collections by Guy Davenport, Stephen Dixon, Jack Matthews, Jean McGarry, and a dozen others. Three months later I had an acceptance and phoned Nat with the good news, assuring him he'd get his 15 percent, since he'd surely tried his best and run up considerable expenses in the process.

With its publication by Johns Hopkins University Press, *Short Season*'s fortunes changed. The press reported a record number of advance orders; the prepublication reviews were strong, and at publication (in time for Opening Day of the 1988 baseball season), a remarkable number of positive reviews began coming in from big-city newspapers across the country. This prompted paperback interest, to the extent that Johns Hopkins had not only their first subsidiary sale from the series but was able to conduct it as an auction—a nice bit of revenge, since all six houses bidding had rejected the book in hardcover. Meanwhile, the press's own sales were strong enough to prompt another first for the series, a second printing. When the paperback did appear a year later with Macmillan, I saw it everywhere. On their own, my students found out about it and asked that it be added to our course.

And so as a teacher and critic, rather than just as author, I would have a chance to consider just why the book had failed so miserably as a novel and then, with a few strokes of opaquing fluid, became a success as a short story collection. My introductory course for general education was a good place for such investigation, for instead of asking students to passively accept the great canonical literary books, we choose a range of current works and study them less for their aesthetic and moral import than for the technical and rhetorical structures by which they function, literally taking them apart and putting them back together again in a way the more enshrined bodies of literary tradition would resist, given all the assumptions of excellence and authority. What we found in *Short Season* was much that I'd presumed, but also a great deal more—things that I hadn't been aware of when planning the book as a novel but that in the format of interconnected narratives highlighted both a rhythm of action and an evolving pattern of disruptions, constraints, and finally resolutions. All that was present in the novel, of course, but was structurally obstructed by the novel-reader's frustrated desire for the continuous development of a central character within a narratively logical context. As a story collection, my book could now invite the reader to see the chance for a somewhat modified context every six or ten or twenty pages; it would be those contexts that accrued and not just details of character or developed action—not a big fish swimming through the sea but the effect of wave after wave meeting the shore, each with its slightly different nature but building in sum toward a totality of effect.

As such, *Short Season*'s twenty-eight stories (covering 187 pages) fall quite naturally into six movements—just a half dozen because after a couple of semesters that turned out to be the comfortable number of classes over which to teach the book. My pet theory has been that in a new work the author uses the first pages to provide instructions on how to read it, sometimes overtly, usually through subtle promptings. My own first stories, "Pregame" and "Short Season," handle the task as a problem: By introducing the structure of the game and how it is played and watched, readers can surmise all the possibilities for subsequent action. The hour during which the stands are open before each game allows for preparation, on field and off, from raking the infield to buying hot dogs and beer. As the players warm up and the fans settle down, I could introduce the half dozen of each who would become prominent in later stories; here the reader would not only meet them but also learn about them in their context. Yet as "Pregame," the story has its own integrity, for pregame preparations are an activity in themselves. So too is the earlier-afternoon business of the manager, which I detailed in the second story, "Short Season," spatially structured so as to introduce the reader to the ballpark's physical dimensions as the skipper walks the outfield, inspects the infield, frets about the cramped dugouts and low tunnel, and then makes his way through the lockers and trainer's room into the stadium's most insulated realm, his office, where he settles down to write the day's reports. Here I used a trick—an intrasyntactic device helpful for shifting point of view in order to transcend boundaries of time and space—that was taught to me by Richard Yates. As manager Carl Peterson sits down at his desk, the mountains of paperwork strike him as materials for a novel, dealing as they do with the interesting personalities readers have met in the story before. "Why not," he muses, "he's got good enough stories already to fill a book." There's an hour of tedium ahead, however, as he prepares to complete the player reports to his boss, the farm club director of the Kansas City Royals. But first, one last moment of musing:

> Posted on a wall is a jumbo postcard Carl's daughter has sent him from Paris on her junior year abroad, showing scattered rooftops sloping down the Left Bank toward the Seine. He gazes out across them before turning back to his desk. Old Ernie Hemingway, he thinks to himself, that's who I really am, as he wonders what brilliant story to concoct tonight for his boss in Kansas City.

As the postcard becomes Carl's window not just overlooking Paris but as an invitation to literary opportunity, the collection's action gets underway—with a disruption, just as the normal course of vision has been disrupted by that two-dimensional postcard turning into the viewpoint Hemingway enjoyed each morning from his rented room on the rue Descartes. With this second movement we have a group of stories devoted to all the possibilities for disruption: from the horseplay during a rain delay and the ribbing that takes place during batting practice to the worries of the club's general manager and the chance that a budding friendship between the Panamanian shortstop and a young girl working as a shagger may be flirting with the boundaries of sex.

But a short story collection cannot be all disruption, all collision. And so the stories from "Ball Two" through "Five Bad Hands and the Wild Mouse Folds" concentrate less on disruption than on the path it takes; these are stories more about system than content. Then, in a fourth movement running from "Workouts" through "Costy Pedraza's Greatest Pitch," the emphasis is shifted from disruption itself and the paths it can take to the measures of its containment. Consider the nature of "Bus Trip," in which a beer-guzzling septuagenarian with a lead foot on the accelerator makes each road trip a nightmare of anticipated bus crashes. Yet for all its action, the focus is not on the driver or the bus but rather on the manager, whose worry fills the pages with metaphor and conspires to limit the driver's misbehavior.

These four movements fill just the first third of the book, but already thirteen of twenty-eight stories have taken place. The shifts in rhythm and pacing, I can see now, are what get the larger narrative moving while still covering introductory material. Like a player warming up, the reader is now both exercised and familiar with the lay of the field. We know about what can happen at second base, so now there's time and space for a longer, more relaxed story out there. And so forth around the diamond, through the park, and out into the larger world that holds these fans and players. For the book's last two-thirds, the stories get longer and the moods are more sustained—for good reason, because rather than disruption and attempts at containment, *Short Season* is now devoting itself to the depths of memory and feeling. It is here that two players spend a whole story musing about the sounds of a ballpark; another player is released; the old pitching coach reaches into his past for a bag of tricks and a sheaf of reminiscences about baseball of another day; a sportswriter responds to all of this with a rash of colorful metaphors, anticipating the collection's resolution; and two players take off for quick visits home, one in triumph, the other in self-induced failure.

This fifth movement, of memory and emotion, blends into the sixth and conclusive grouping of stories, those that emphasize the role of imagination in grasping the nature of minor league baseball's short season. A fan gets to exercise his fantasies playing outfield during batting practice; the workout exceeds his abilities to keep up, but so do the fantasies it engenders. From here to the end, other bits and pieces of the imagination complete our dimensions of the game, until the book concludes with "Gametime," a full-circle progress from "Pregame," with the season having come to its conclusion and the reader treated to the collection's first full account of a baseball game as played. As the championship contest, it makes for a natural climax in terms of action. But what carries the narrative is the winning pitcher's imagination, which ranges through not just the entire summer but his whole life as he pitches the classic perfect game, an ideal to which all twenty-eight stories have been impending, just as does every baseball game ever played.

Why couldn't *Short Season* be a novel? Because of the anti-novelistic nature of its material, of course: As opposed to the majors, a minor league season lacks the focus and continuity a novel requires. Yet there is a style of development present in minor league baseball, and for it an integrated collection of stories seems natural. Action comes in disparate bits and pieces, from all different directions; the game is smaller and less consequential but also more accessible, and because of that, its dimensions are multipled rather than compressed. A major league season is sufficiently continuous and so integral that one can digest it in larger chunks, but in the minors you really have to catch a little bit of it every night. The focus is diverse and shifting; it is better not trying to run too much of it together.

The joy of it, however, is to ease on out to the park every night and settle into its comfortable surroundings. Much will be the same, but a few things will be different- for example, a new player up from the rookie league to replace a star just promoted to Double A. That roster change can make for several stories, from new allegiances in the clubhouse to an abandoned girlfriend in town. The fans will talk about these aspects even as they watch the new kid on the field and wonder who will now carry the star's missing weight. Next week, the fans will know a bit more about these problems, but there will be new developments as well. And so it goes throughout the short season from April through August, to which the genuinely novelistic conclusion of the major league season in September is merely a disinterested coda. As for winners and losers, so memorable in the majors, few may remember who won last year's minor league crown, for the point has been enjoying the presence of baseball down here and not its somewhat artificial spectacle of contrived success.

Whether *Short Season* succeeds as a story collection is the reader's judgment, not mine. But I do know that what I expect from a good book of stories is replicated in the habits I found so comfortable in minor league baseball. Going out to the game each night is somewhat like curling up with a good book of stories, a promise of both novelty and familiarity. When a writer I truly admire, such as Grace Paley, Steve Dixon, or Rob Wilson, publishes a new collection, I savor it the same way: one story each night. As opposed to the experience of reading a novel, which can range from an ongoing, unstoppable rush to the tedium of banging away at a bulk of pages that seemingly never ends, a good short story collection promises anywhere from a dozen to two dozen nice little reading experiences, as firmly scheduled yet individually unpredictable as a set of minor league baseball games. Each has its pleasures. Neither is big league. But in view of the rewards offered, who would want it to be?

Inside the World Series:
An Outsider's Notes

YOU got these tickets," the fan beside me asked, "because
you know somebody, huh?" Game three of the 1982 World
Series was half an hour from getting under way. The St.
Louis Cardinals were just starting to trickle out of the visitors' dugout here at Milwaukee County Stadium, where in about
ten minutes they and the Brewers would line up along the basepaths to be introduced. The game they'd play would be the first
such contest between pennant winners in my old home town
since the Braves faced the Yankees in 1958.

At age fourteen I'd have given anything to be sitting here,
back when my baseball enthusiasm was at a peak. As a nine-year-
old, I'd been the right person in the right place at the right time
when the Boston Braves moved in and made us all big league. By
'58, when this upstart team in a small-townish city proved their
power by contending with the grandest franchise in the land, I
was big enough to feel rightfully swept along. It was great to be
a fan then, just like the lucky fellow next to me was probably
feeling right now.

Indeed, he was grinning like a possum eating candy as I told
him yes, I knew somebody. He didn't want to know who, and I
was glad he didn't try to guess, as trying to explain how I owned

part of a minor league baseball team never made for easy introductions at other ballparks, unless everyone was already three
sheets to the wind. The ownership perk was what got me here:
Our general manager back in Waterloo secured three tickets to
each of the Milwaukee games from our parent club, Cleveland,
which was enough of a poor relation among major league organizations to happily sell off its allotment of Series tickets to anyone
who'd pay. And so here I was perched at the edge of Cleveland's
seating block. In the rows ahead, I recognized a few of the big
outfit's coaches who during the 1981 strike had come down to
see their A club in the Midwest League. Some folks closer were
probably involved in the Indians' other minor league affiliates at
Tacoma, Chattanooga, and Batavia, Cleveland's respective entries
in the Pacific Coast, Southern, and New York-Penn Leagues. But
with me was where the influence drained down to practically
nothing, for to my right was this typical Milwaukeean, Packer
stocking cap and all, who'd cashed in by having his luck-of-the-
draw mail order filled. He must have thought he was the only guy
in the park who wasn't somebody or somebody's friend.

In fifty-five-thousand seat County Stadium, he wasn't. But
the impression still held that this was a big-time show meant for
television and the history books and that viewing it in person was
reserved for folks with privilege or clout. Up to twenty thousand
tickets for such an event are assigned to Major League Baseball:
for their bigwigs, employees, and people they want to impress. Or,
as in Cleveland's case, to sell for some needed revenue. Given that
the home team's season ticket holders have first dibs on their own
seats, a small house like Chicago's Wrigley Field or Fenway Park
in Boston can be filled up pretty fast. Back in '57 and '58, with
the Milwaukee ballpark yet to be enlarged and the cost of such a
ticket well beyond my reach, I could only watch it between Gil-
lette commercials on TV, even though this world class event was
taking place just a few miles from my home, in a stadium to
which I'd been paying an unremarkable $1.25 (adult!) general
admission all summer. Now, almost a quarter century and half a
lifetime later, with two half-grown children of my own in tow as

testimony to all this intervening time, I was part of the event myself, seated next to the one true fan of 1982 who thought himself right to be the only normal person around.

And how right he was. Everything seemed larger than life, from Joe Garagiola standing there at the pregame batting cage resplendent in male-pattern baldness to the Goodyear blimp droning overhead. My son and daughter didn't understand why I wanted to linger down in the lower boxes, cruising aisles near the field to be close to the media circus. NBC cameras, outstanding with their fan of color, were positioned everywhere, as were recognizable faces: Commissioner Bowie Kuhn, Brewers owner Bud Selig, Tony Kubek doing a pregame interview with manager Harvey Kuenn, Whitey Herzog over next to the Cards' dugout with Johnny Bench from CBS Radio, plus some of the old Milwaukee broadcasters I recalled from Braves days.

Ushers would politely ask us to keep moving, embarrassing the kids with their oddly behaving father. But I insisted that we hang on down there until a buzzer from the Brewers' bench signaled it was time to clear the field. The big names like Kubek and Garagiola exited through the dugouts, but with the line of others now coming up through the field gates, an eerie thing took place. As reporters, baseball people, and some small-time personalities filed by, dozens of faceless people who'd been milling there in the walkways suddenly took shape and voice.

"Buy your press pin?" one would murmur to those sporting the 1982 Series logo on their lapels. "Sell your field pass?" another would query, audible just under the breath. I didn't see anyone comply. But it was odd being in a crowd of such seekers, like zombies grasping for a ticket to real life. No wonder my kids had felt out of place in this group. They'd surely sensed it long before I did: that in a world where their own proper role was to sit down and enjoy the performance about to be staged, certain figures felt compelled to step through the screen, as it were, to engage themselves in the spectacle that by virtue of its spotlighted drama spoke of existence more genuine than their own.

Up in our seats, we entered yet another world. The location

was what you'd describe as okay, thirty rows up about halfway between home and first. The upper deck loomed over us, keeping everything in shadows and making the blimp just a disembodied roar that from time to time enveloped the stadium as it passed overhead for a TV shot. Better than nosebleed seats for sure, but a long way from the front tier of boxes one always yearns for (and where I could sit anytime I wanted to in our own underpatronized minor league ballpark back home). I was glad enough to have them, good enough seats when the team was drawing and reminiscent of where I'd sat on the opposite side in 1953 when the park sold out almost every night and my father had used brewery connections to get us to my first ball game.

In retrospect, I guess that's the level of excitement I was looking for at Game Three of the 1982 World Series. I must have figured that it would be a way of making good on what my parents had hoped for: that I'd grow up decent and sound and capable of taking my own kids to a baseball game at Milwaukee County Stadium—a World Series game, no less. No matter that the kids took it all as a matter of course. They'd already seen Paris and London, whereas it took me 'til twice their age to ever cross the border into Canada. There's progress in generations, as one always hopes. Here at the Series, I'd have been happy enough for the excitement to be my own. But as with the zombies who made me question my own motives in being down there trying to taste the thrill of the field, the crowd I was sitting in did not make for a customarily enjoyable game. Except for Happy Fan, who followed each play with a semblance of interest, no one around me seemed much concerned with action between the lines.

Not that there wasn't action to comment on. In the rows just below me, there was much coming and going, all of it orchestrated by gestures and cautiously shared asides. Stately Dave Duncan was the one I kept noticing. A year before, when as a strike-idled Indians pitching coach he'd visited Waterloo to survey our mound staff, I'd been struck by how much he looked like the immensely more famous Don Drysdale. Now, with Cleveland's ownership and management in transition, he was one of several dozen employees wondering about their jobs. From coaches and scouts to farm system staff and front office types, everyone from Dave on down had to be sure things were lined up for the 1983 season, a year that might or might not find them in Cleveland. Who knew? Well, the brass behind Bowie Kuhn in the bannered and buntinged field seats did, and it was on them that Dave Duncan's and the others' attention was focused.

Over three days, an interesting rhythm developed. Before each game there was the atmosphere of preliminary festivity, something in which the whole city took part. The kids and I knew this would be happening, from the day before when, just like the teams on their travel date from St. Louis, we drove up from Cedar Falls to my mother's home in suburban Greenfield. As usual for our Milwaukee trips, I tuned in WTMJ—"*The Milwaukee Journal* station," my hometown's last unpostmodernized radio outlet—as soon as we could reach its signal, and all across southwestern Wisconsin, we listened to the usual corniness of *Ask Your Neighbor* and other homey shows. Most times it would be Gordon Hinkley fielding a call about "How can I get a pepperoni stain off my white poof rug?" by responding "Beats me—but maybe somebody out there knows," letting the show roll on through hour after hour of southside accents that delighted the kids as reminders of how their own Polish-American relatives spoke.

This day, however, Gordon had fallen into the snares of a listener who'd asked him to play some classic rock tunes that could be associated with current Brewers players. What followed had the kids rolling with laughter in the back seat—not just because the ancient-sounding songs were so funny, such as "Rockin' Robin" for Robin Yount, "Oh Paul, Oh Paula" for Paul Molitor, and "Big Boy Pete" celebrating six-six reliever Peter Ladd, but for the unself-conscious enthusiasm of these Milwaukeeans for their True Blue Brew Crew. Only much farther on in the decade would a more jaded team see these fans gathering for a welcome home at the airport and say, "Look at all the cheeseheads," coining a name local folks still wear with misconstrued pride. The whole scene of brew-town baseball and its clumsy fans was summed up by bad-boy Jeffrey Leonard, who when being traded from the Giants to the Brewers gave the most patently deconstructive interview line of all times: "Personal achievement means nothing— I just want to join the team and help bring a pennant to Milwaukee, wherever the hell *that* is."

Heading to County Stadium the next day, we couldn't help but see how the World Series had monopolized attention. At the end of every downtown avenue's perspective, it seemed, loomed the Goodyear blimp, making my old hometown look like newsreel clips from the Hindenberg disaster. Roads leading to the ballpark were jammed, but not by ticket holders, twenty thousand of whom were Major League insiders and arriving by taxi, limo, and chartered bus from the hotels. Rather the traffic stream was for tailgaters, tens of thousands of whom would pay ten dollars for otherwise unused parking spots in County Stadium's lot and the customary Brewer pregame activity of beer-bust partying (only now it would be something that carried on all game long).

Which didn't surprise me, and was why we'd rented a car in Cedar Falls rather than bring our family sedan to town. In typical Milwaukee fashion, the practice wasn't even native or traditional. Instead, it was something borrowed from what Green Bay Packer fans up in West DePere did to keep warm before frigid November football games, which the Minneapolis fans at old Metropolitan Stadium adopted back when Twins baseball was struggling to establish itself in a world dedicated to basketball, hockey, and ice fishing. At County Stadium in Milwaukee, the practice was designed to hassle purists the worst. Come early to watch batting practice and you'd have to park in the middle of a beer and bratwurst blowout, charcoal grills roaring to life two feet away from your car's gas tank. Before you and your kids were in the gate, your pristine vehicle would be a picnic bench.

As it turned out, my fears were more than justified. Over the three-game sequence, our nondescript Hertz rental fared no worse than a couple baths of beer and one of vomit, but on our way out after the second contest I got a view of one poor soul's coming nightmare: Some clowns in a jacked-up monster four-by-four had parked close by a beautiful low-slung Jaguar and were using its roof as a grilling platform.

Under the new Milwaukee rubrics, this type of stuff was encouraged, the more cavemanlike the better. Bud Selig's ball club sold tickets to it as an end in itself; television stations sent in live remotes, covering "the party atmosphere." There were no more fears of looking bush league, as Milwaukee Braves fans had worried when hosting the New York Yankees back in 1957 and 1958. Instead, the city had elected to foreground its thickness in a never-ending series of "fests." Because by traditional German Oktoberfest time it was too cold up here to celebrate outdoors, the city now mounted Italian Fest in May, Irish Fest in June, and so forth at almost weekly intervals through late spring and summer. For Italian Fest, you'd tailgate, put on a red hat, and drink lots of Miller beer while bands boomed out heavy metal rock music. The same bands and drinkers would be back for Irish Fest, everyone now wearing green hats. One August we'd tried visiting the zoo and found its grounds taken over by Zoo Fest, with polar bears, elephants, and all the other animals terrorized by blaring headbanger music. The beer itself came in 128-ounce buckets, which festgoers would throw on one another. World Series Fest had been a long time coming, but here it was with a vengeance.

Inside the park, however, matters were more serious. True, there was some beer throwing in the back rows well behind me, in the few seats available to True Blue Brew Crew fans. But from my area on down, the atmosphere was deadly businesslike. I noticed this from the first Brewer hit. Not only were there not a lot of cheers, but among the Cleveland personnel in front of me hardly anyone looked up. Heads remained buried in studied conversation, with occasional worried glances at the boxes between the dugouts. At one point when the Cardinals had the bases loaded and I was hanging on every Brewer pitch, Dave Duncan leapt up, dashed to the front row seats, and squatted in the aisle next to a jowly looking man who'd just come in. In a few minutes he was back, sharing information with those on either side.

Weren't the Winter Meetings for things like this? Other

board members from our minor league club in Waterloo had gone south to attend them and came back loaded with promotional items and tales about rubbing shoulders with the likes of Yogi Berra, Peter O'Malley, and Hank Aaron. Guys like that already had jobs, I figured, or didn't need them. Imagine how desperate those hallways, bars, and coffee shops must be during the first days of December, when anyone like Dave Duncan not yet hired might well spend the next season selling cars or insurance. No wonder he was concentrating so hard now on the eve of this year's hot stove league, when baseball's most crucial business would be conducted.

Which prompted me to alter baseball history. By the third and last game in Milwaukee, I'd become fed up with the job market being worked so distractingly between my seat and the action on the field. The unemployed pitching coach had moved up a few rows closer as he conspired with other Clevelanders past and present. Because the people just in front of me were away from their seats, the seventh inning stretch found Dave and myself standing just a few feet apart. He was scanning the crowd back here as if looking for a special face, and for some reason his glance caught mine.

I was *somebody*. Or I *knew* somebody. A year ago he would have seen me during his prolonged travels around the organization, and now I could tell he was trying to remember *where*. Was it someplace *important*?

Still talking with the person next to him, he stayed turned around and let me hear what he was saying, something to the effect that he'd do this or that "if it's Lucchesi." *Frank Lucchesi.* I'd read this feisty old-timer was a candidate for manager, but that was all, nothing special about it or corresponding to anything I knew. Not that this could stop me now.

"It's Lucchesi," I announced, entering the conversation with a steadfastly level stare at Dave Duncan. His colleague twisted around, surprised by this voice out of nowhere. Dave, however, stayed as solid as myself.

"You think so?" he asked, eyebrows raised halfway between skepticism and real curiosity.

"I *know* so," I said, and sat back down with the crowd. Gorman Thomas would be hitting soon, and this might be the last time I'd see him other than on TV. I had just two-and-a-half innings left of live World Series baseball, and I was determined to enjoy them. By the time I looked back, Dave was gone.

As history now records, it wasn't Frank Lucchesi. Pat Corrales became the new Cleveland Indians manager. Having taken a bum lead and wasted it on the wrong candidate, Dave Duncan wound up elsewhere, coaching an Oakland Athletics mound staff to its best performance in years, making a genius and perennial World Series manager out of Tony LaRussa. But for the moment he was out of my hair. The only guy more relieved was Happy Fan, who'd just guessed who I knew.

Two innings later, things got bad again. I'd asked the kids to hold off on souvenirs until we were leaving, so as not to be lugging junk around all during the game. I'd hoped to find vendors outside the stadium, but it turned out you could only get the official stuff inside. That seemed an extra nuisance but essentially okay, as the program and Series yearbook were removed from mass-marketing business to be kept special for the game itself. I thought of all the stuff one of my fellow board members displayed in her basement, not just baseball cards and programs from college basketball's Final Four but such things as a liter of Pepsi brought home from Iowa's appearance in the Peach Bowl, a "special limited edition" available only on site. A hundred years from now, if the sports collector craze continued, we both guessed it would be worth more than a similarly vintaged bottle of rare French wine.

What I now learned was that the market for this stuff didn't have to wait one hundred years. Avoiding all the pandemonium directly beneath the stands, I led the kids down to a more open area where fans such as I'd once been entered the right field section, County Stadium's traditional cheap seats. There'd always been a souvenir counter down here, and happily there still was. And not even a terrible line, just three or four ahead of me. Sample items strung overhead showed what was available, so I told the kids to start thinking: one big item or a couple of small ones apiece. For myself, I wanted the available literature, which meant Dad would pig out with more things for himself, plus maybe an official Series baseball, if neither Jonathan nor Nina chose that.

Ten minutes later we were still standing there looking up, for the line hadn't moved at all. After another few minutes, I could see why: People hadn't been buying just a thing or two but were doing all they could to break the bank. Finally, when there was just one guy ahead of me, I could grasp the immensity of such a project.

This fellow was no cheesehead or even someone like me, a long lost son come home. No sir, this guy wasn't dressed like any Milwaukeean, past or present. Camel hair coat, cut to a fashionable car length; snappy fedora; sharply tailored slacks; even alligator shoes. Had anyone tried throwing beer on him, there would have been all hell to pay. And here he was, a massive choker of fifty- and hundred-dollar bills in his hand, peeling dozens off his wad to pay for various bags being stuffed. Twenty World Series baseball caps in one, a big stack of Brewers and Cardinals championship pennants in another. Box after box of Series balls. Thousands of dollars were changing hands before me, with no sign of stopping. Would there be anything left by the time he was done?

My question was soon answered. "You out of scorecards, programs, and yearbooks?" he asked the concessions clerk, and when told yes said, "Okay, gimme those." Away went the display copies I'd been watching for the past half hour.

There were things left like wristbands and Brewer figures and other regular season merchandise, and from this the kids picked out what they wanted, neither knowing about nor caring for the distinction. Meanwhile, stadium security was finding a cart for Mr. Big Spender, who probably would have been happy to resell the display booklets right then and there. I've never bothered to check what they're bringing on the collectibles market these days but can easily imagine.

Outside, the crowd was worse than ever. Tailgaters still clogged the parking lots, making it impossible for anyone to drive. Yet who would want to? After this, the party would be over. Who knew when the Brewers would win another pennant. Who knew even how long Milwaukee could hold a major league team, as small and as closed in as its market was. Radio and television stations were broadcasting live from the stadium's sidewalks, pumping up the crowd wedged between the exiting crush and the parking lot parties still going full tilt.

It was late, well past a responsible time for getting the kids home. So we'd drive through some tailgate parties—that's why we had a rental. But getting out of the stadium concourse would be the first problem.

I'm pretty good at getting through a crowd and can make my wife mad at me for unobtrusively slipping us ahead in lines. The secret is moving slowly, so that no one quite realizes you're doing it, but also making your progress semi-laterally, opening up cracks at forty-five degrees to the left, then forty-five degrees to the right. Suddenly you're way up in front of the guy who used to be ahead of you, but because there are half a dozen people in between, he'll never notice and squawk.

Soon I'd eased myself and my kids to the walkway's edge, where after just a few more feet we could start making our way between cars to where our party-spattered rental was waiting. (Folks holding drinks are easier to thread your way through, as bent arms create several extra inches of slither-space.) But here we came up against a different kind of obstacle: a police officer, helmeted for the occasion, who was trying to hold the crowd back.

He looked a little worried, which is a bad image for any cop to project. Consequently, fans were getting jostled against him and were kidding about why didn't he ease up, let them through, and come along himself to crash some of the tailgate blasts.

Pressure from behind brought me face to face with him. At six-four and near two hundred pounds, I must have looked like a threat, half a head above him. Careful to rid my voice of any Milwaukee accent I might have reacquired this past half week, I spoke to him quietly, like the ally I truly felt I was.

"Where are you getting us to go?" I asked, showing how eager I was to turn collaborationist against this crowd of what can only be called "sports fans."

"We want to clear a way from here in a line toward that light pole," he answered gratefully, indicating the direction with his eyes.

As he looked that way, I glanced back the other and saw a big black limo nosing out from a service gate but unable to make its way much farther through the crowd.

"The commissioner?" I asked, wondering who else but Bowie Kuhn would merit such treatment.

"On the nosey," the cop replied, glad that I was leaning back and getting those on either side of me to do the same. Meanwhile I could see a mounted policeman moving ahead of Kuhn's chariot to guide it through the fray.

"Turn around," the cop muttered, and to my uncomprehending stare, gave me a quick, candid explanation. "To save your toes—that's how the equestrian patrol will open things up."

It was great to finally get back to my mother's, even nicer to return to Cedar Falls. But just before winding things up, there was one last stop to make: at Waterloo Municipal Stadium, where in his rathole of a general manager's office Marshall Adesman was at his desk, already planning sales campaigns to promote next year's minor league season.

After much colder than usual weather in Milwaukee, it had warmed back up to some nice Indian-summerish temperatures. Even though we were travel weary and anxious to get home, I wanted to impose on the kids to do a little more—to have them walk up the ramp with me to see our own little ball field spread out beneath the sky, to amble along the aisle behind the double row of lower boxes until we reached our own, between home plate and the on-deck circle.

More than five months would have to pass before our Waterloo Indians could have another game here, and very few of the intervening days would be as pleasant as this one. But first there was Marshall to thank.

"Hey," I told our general manager as we piled into his tiny office, "I never knew!"

"Never knew what?" he asked.

"That you were somebody," I replied, letting him smile with the satisfaction of knowing what I meant.

On the Grass

THE great romantics of baseball writing have made much of the ball field's sacred, almost mystical nature—how right within the overbuilt clutter of gridlocked urban America can be found a clean, green acreage of pastoral splendor, nothing but three canvas sacks, a rubberized plate, and two lime-chalked lines added to its natural grass and dirt. Even for today's suburbanized stadiums, fans must drive through freeway traffic, get bottlenecked into measured parking stalls, then trek across tundras of asphalt and wend their way through concrete tunnels before getting that first breathtaking view of the field's oasis, set off so specially from all that surrounds.

For me, the special thrill has not been that first glimpse of the grass but walking down to it, loitering in the aisle along the lower boxes and looking back up to grasp the immensity of all that encloses it. The stadium, raked back and looming up with one or two decks towering over the field. The people, anywhere from thirty to sixty thousand of them, accompanied by tiers of news media ranked along the mezzanine. Television cameras pointed down from all angles. Perhaps even airplanes pulling banners, advertising to the assemblage below. All of this just to focus on the green enclosure separated by a low, not even waist-high wall.

But a wall that draws the absolute line between the climax of everything outside from this very special area within.

The finality of that line is printed on the ticket that lets you in. "Anyone interfering with the ball in play or entering the field will be ejected and subject to prosecution," the legal warning reads. Cross that line and you disappear, hauled out of the ballpark and stricken from the television screen, which will happily show you doing anything else, from catching a foul ball to waving a banner or just looking photogenic. Ownership of that baseball changes once it crosses into the seats. But throw something back and you're ostracized; getting down on the field itself is made to seem totally unimaginable. The field, after all, is where special things are done by unique people, the whole reason for having this arena.

Yet what makes the line so fascinating is that there are occasional tiny openings in it, places where from time to time people other than ballplayers can get through. Hence the attraction to loitering down there, looking for that once in a million break.

The first time I came across one such fissure stunned me. As a nine-year-old fan of the newly arrived 1953 Milwaukee Braves, it was impossible to get anywhere close to the action: I was too small, and the hullabaloo over the team was much too big. But just two years later I could take the convenient train to Chicago and see my heroes as an unexceptionable road team at Wrigley Field, mostly empty for a rainy day midweek game.

Box seats for kids cost next to nothing, and the ticket seller found me one just a few rows behind the Braves dugout. From here it was not even a question of loitering: The line and its environs were my turf to enjoy as I pleased. A few others were here to take the same privilege, and before me in the front row was a man at the wall, just next to the dugout. Walking up behind him, I could see what was up.

To my shocked amazement, he had found a breach and was actually leaning through it, piercing the plane between two worlds. Leaning from the opposite side was a player—Braves first baseman Joe Adcock—who looked just as remarkable for what he was doing, reaching ever so slightly into the realm meant not for action but for observation. Drama critics call it the stage's invisible but impenetrable fourth wall. Theologians honor the same principle by citing the rarity of beatific visions, art historians by referencing Michelangelo's Sistine Chapel depiction of God reaching to Adam with the touch of life, the kind of thing that happens only once in a world's existence. Here it was happening right before me: Adcock's burly arms at rest on the low wall, his head and the fan's nodded forward to meet in a dialogue between two otherwise discrete dimensions.

Plus there was physical evidence of this meeting. On the fan's scorecard was Joe's autograph, distinctive as the patented stamp on the machine-signed balls I'd purchased for each year's team. Except this was the real thing.

Searching out my pen and turning my scorecard to a proper page, I took my eyes off the scene before me. A moment later, when I looked up, it was gone. The fan was walking away behind me, and Joe Adcock had disappeared. This wasn't a line for autographs, like at a player's appearance at a gas station or grocery store promotion. No—the curtain had parted for a moment, and now it was closed. The figure over at first base taking throws and the occasional grounder for infield practice was once again a creature utterly beyond reach.

For the next twenty-some years, that was as close as I got. Even when the Braves' great popularity died down, they still drew better than the Cubs, especially for the hardcore circle of field boxes on top of the action. At Comiskey Park, where I'd train down to see the White Sox, ushers were more dutiful about keeping kids away from that privileged realm where the likes of Al Capone and these days Mayor Daley could be seen kibitzing with Luke Appling or Nellie Fox. Then after 1965, the Braves themselves were taken from me, and I soured on baseball for more than a decade.

By the time I returned a dozen years later, a lot of things had changed. I was grown up with kids of my own and living hundreds of miles away, out in Iowa where the ball was minor league and the dimensions a whole bunch more intimate. Yet even in the comparatively tiny ballpark where I'd begun taking the kids, the barrier between stands and field was real. True, it was easier to talk to players, and anyone could buy a front row seat for just a few dollars. But the line was as absolute as ever. Even down here, it was treated as a great ceremony when someone was invited out to throw the first pitch or honor a player at home plate with a community award. Tickets carried the same dire warning, and even though foul balls had to be returned to the usher, it was with the sense of a hostage being redeemed, fans getting a free drink and hot dog for returning this fugitive object from another, utterly different world.

Hence it was with great excitement that I received an invitation to join the club's board of directors. Financially, it was no big deal, as the team was a break-even operation run by unpaid civic volunteers. Yet the players were real professionals, farm system prospects of the Cleveland Indians, and the games were treated with the same respect as everything else that wound up enshrined in the records at Cooperstown.

What happened on the field remained administratively separate from off-field activities. None of the dozen-and-a-half board members, who were in fact the club's owners, had anything to do with what happened beyond the line. My own duties were typical: selling season tickets in the preseason, helping clean up the stadium for opening day, filling in at the beer bar for a few innings during heavily attended games, and meeting monthly for business decisions. After running the stadium operation, the closest our work got to the players was leasing a bus for road games and arranging their motels. If a player got sent up or down, we booked the airline ticket and were reimbursed by the front office in Cleveland. Our general manager would distribute meal money in little packets before each series of games away but spent most of his time selling advertising, booking promotions, riding herd on the concessions staff, and turning off the lights each night before locking up. Three or four times a year we'd have a picnic for the players, who'd huddle amongst themselves in timid groups. Just a few became intimates of board members who may have lent them furniture or helped their wives get summer jobs. But not even these few folks were privileged to get down on the field. The special relationships they shared with their specific ballplayers were conducted through the backstop screen reinforcing the line, a line that even owning the team did not empower one to cross.

Who did get through? One of our board members was Russ Smith, sports editor for the Waterloo *Courier*. That's how civic we were: It was no conflict of interest for the game's chief journalist to help run the team he was covering. Yet his reporter's credentials were a mantle of sorts, a cloak he could don that let him pass from civilian life into the world of uniformed players and umpires. Before each game, he'd descend from the press box, waddle down the aisle, and with notebook in hand, make his way onto the field and disappear into each dugout for the lineups. Sometimes he'd get even closer to the action, standing behind the batting cage for some info from the manager as he watched tonight's hitters take their practice swings.

Russ's posture in this whole affair spoke for a separation of its own. He was, after all, someone important: not just a writer but a sports editor, in that position for over thirty years. As I say, he waddled—a big man, heftily overweight, off balance with an out-of-place hip and cursed with poor sight as well, quite literally blind in one eye and not able to see well out of the other. His proximity to the game didn't excite him. Quite the contrary. Long service had made it just another job, and his attitude after the first out was to sigh, "Okay, fifty-three more to go." No, Russ Smith's ability to pass through baseball's invisible but absolute wall wasn't by itself something to impress me.

What did was how some of the other sportswriters approached their work. To my own responsibilities, I'd added the invented role of press officer. By reading the sports papers, researching record books, and combing the daily stats reports, I was able to supply the press box with a steady stream of sidelights, perhaps a player's number in the draft or where he played college ball. If a visiting pitcher was a number one pick from Iowa State, for example, even sleepy old Russ Smith was likely to take notice and use it in his story. When younger writers had the game, there was a better market for what I could provide, from how a hitter did last year in the rookie leagues to what his slugging percentage was against this particular visiting team. Doug Newhoff appreciated the college data, and Jim Sullivan liked knowing whether someone had a streak going or was wearing the collar more often than not. Don Kruse, who covered the Waterloo Indians almost as often as did Russ Smith, was the most eager of all and also knew the most about my information, right down to talking knowledgably about high school baseball records and reputations—"the preps," as he liked to call them.

Kruse was equally enthusiastic about crossing over into baseball's sacred territory. He was forever in the dugout, out on the bull pen bench, in the locker room, or around the batting cage, gathering what he could from manager, coaches, and players but mostly just enjoying being down there on the grass. A few years later my friend Jerry Rosen told how his own buddy Barry Gifford would finagle a press pass just for that sensation. For Gifford, it wasn't the hobnobbing or even getting near where the players were. No, with credentials from a San Francisco paper, he'd make his way over to Oakland Coliseum well before the A's game time and let himself through the gate, taking a position a few steps beyond the box seat wall. *On the grass*, that was what mattered. Just one step over the line, but a crucial step indeed.

What tickled me the most about Don Kruse was one of the first sights I had of him during that initial summer of minor league games when I was still learning the ropes. It was out in front of the dugout during that ten or fifteen minutes of dead time, after batting and infield practice have concluded and everyone, except the starting pitchers warming up in the bull pens, is lolling around before the game. This is the time when batboys, nine-year-olds in our case, might convince an infielder or outfielder to play a little catch. It makes for a happy scene of youngsters with their heroes, playing at being heroes themselves. And right in the middle of it was an overgrown kid with a reporter's notebook sticking out of his hip pocket, tossing a baseball back and forth with a couple of players and grinning enough to be having the time of his life.

Here, I sensed, was an ally in my quest for stepping through the gap between life in the stands and on the field. Finding that Don was most receptive to my background information, I began making more frequent trips to the press box, sometimes lingering for an inning or two to soak up the journalists' atmosphere. One year we had Chuck Stobbs as pitching coach, the old Washington Senators' left hander who didn't look a day younger on his 1952 baseball card than he did now in the 1980s as a grizzled old man. His was the era of names I'd traded as a kid, picking players to be in our games and dealing with their images in each Topps and Bowmans series. That had been Don Kruse's era of boyhood baseball as well, and whenever the game got boring he'd pass along a phony message to Kelly Neff, our PA announcer. Kelly would intone the request for some long dead, obscure American Leaguer to report down at the concessions stand, and Chuck's head, craning like a turkey's, would come leaning out of the dugout, twisted in wonder at these clowns in the press box.

Not that he minded. At least these names of guys he'd played with over thirty years ago were still remembered, and he knew Don savored them as much as the colorfully Hispanic appellations he loved rolling off his tongue in tribute to baseball's new multicultural era. "Costy Pedraza!" Don would shout, liking the name I'd chosen for a character in one of my short stories. "Wayne Terwilliger!" he'd add, oversounding each syllable's linguistic features. "Clyde Kluttz," "Jackie Jensen," "Yo-Yo Davalillo," all of it a litany to the world Chuck Stobbs had played in a seeming lifetime ago, already so old looking when Don and I were little kids.

If ever the fourth dimension of baseball could be found within our three-dimensional world, this was it. My own fiction writing was an attempt to pass beyond such real-life limitations into the artificial, made-up world of sports, but in Don's case he was making baseball join forces with his own existence. Tossing names around with Chuck Stobbs, throwing in one of my fictive players with real stars he'd watched on TV and in person—not to mention doing sidebars and writing game stories that according to the manner he chose would influence how the action was received.

Best of all, from my point of view, was that I could take part in this dimension crossing, feeding Don information and even encouraging the tone of his reporting. One foggy night I got him going on comparisons to *Invasion of the Body Snatchers*, and next day his story was rife with images from that campy horror flick. Another game produced such an exorbitant report that I brought out the clipping next night, stretched comparisons underlined in red, general overwriting noted in green, and a fake 800 listing indicated at the bottom.

"What's that phone number?" Don asked and laughed when I told him.

"It's the metaphor-abuse hotline. Keep it handy for the next time you're tempted."

Of course my friends and I in Box 28 encouraged Don's colorfulness to no end and loved it when one of our own zany metaphors made its way into his copy. Having it turn up in the newspaper was evidence that we ourselves had stepped over for a moment into Don's world, which itself shared turf with what went on among players on the field. The best route through this invisible wall, it turned out, was not a half step forward but all the way back to the press box.

These were the years—the late 1970s and early 1980s—when baseball was getting popular again. Fascination with crossing the line was whetted all the more when the whole country could go nuts over Carlton Fisk urging his World Series homer to stay fair, Reggie Jackson fulfilling the role of Mr. October, Pete Rose closing in on Ty Cobb's all-time hit record, and Nolan Ryan setting strike out records of his own.

My own enthusiasm was already high enough from my involvement with the minors, from helping run the operation to writing the stories that would become *Short Season*. What pushed

me over the edge was getting cable TV just as the Chicago Cubs
hired announcer Harry Caray and the whole mystique of baseball
at Wrigley Field became a national phenomenon.

The appeal of those broadcasts, I've come to believe, is a
carefully orchestrated drama of taking the viewer inside. The routine starts right where my own pregame hauntings would begin,
down at the low brick wall separating seats from field. Here, just a
few feet onto the grass, would be Steve Stone for the pregame show, "down on beautiful Wrigley Field," as he'd introduce
himself each time, occasionally modifying the pitch to make it
seem even more an ongoing process as regular as nature itself—
"down on a very cold but beautiful Wrigley Field," "down on a
hot and humid Wrigley Field," and so forth. It would seem familiar because viewers knew the drill, a drill that continued with
Harry's introduction a few minutes later, his comments addressed
to a shared coterie of friends and places ("Ben Stein . . . Judge
Abraham Lincoln Marovitz . . . Decatur, Illinois, that's Bob Skef-
fington Country, he's the Budweiser distributor down there . . .
and from Peoria, my old friend Pete Vonachen"), plus a customary
run of gags with producer Arne Harris that made viewers feel
even more a part of the gang. For me, catching afternoon games
on WGN was almost like sitting with my friends that night in Box
28 at the Waterloo ballpark. We were all a group of regulars, cozy
with each other's quirks and habits. Harry Caray changed televi-
sion-watching into sitting alongside the most enthusiastic and
familiar fan of all.

Not to mention the voyeurism of nine or ten TV cameras. A
Cubs broadcast, the best televised in all of baseball, not only put
you everywhere but right in the action itself. There were dugout
shots, extreme closeups of the manager, and intimate coverage of
the batter's and pitcher's every nuance. Long shots would take in
the stands from picturesque angles. And all of it in an ever moving but coherent directorial style that made the two-and-a-half
hours of a Cubs telecast a stable, secure experience. Watch them
for a week and you'd begin to recognize the season ticket holders, visible in the alternating closeups of right- and left-handed

hitters. Follow a foul ball into the stands just behind the dugout and spot that day's visiting celebrity. Afterwards, over closing
credits, the camera out in center field would crank back to show
fans leaving the ballpark and making their way through the inter-
section of Clark Street and Waveland Avenue.

The motivation to watch was evident: It was almost like being there. To be there in person would be very nice. But having
become a broadcast intimate of Harry and his world and having
seen everything so close, the best way to do it would be to cross
the line, to get inside—this time inside a world whose special
charms one had sampled as a viewer, again and again until the
real taste to be satisfied became nothing short of a mania.

And so as a baseball kid grown up and as a Cubs cable
watcher to the core, I decided to take advantage of the one avenue my ball club ownership offered me: to have Don Kruse get
us press passes to a Cubs game and take in the show firsthand,
from a position magically across the dividing line. He arranged
them for a May 13 game with San Francisco, well enough before
the summer vacation period where now-fashionable Wrigley
would be overcrowded to the point of discomfort. In recent years
I'd made several day trips to Chicago with my kids and a couple
of Box 28 regulars and had the pattern down with ease. Get up
early, leave by 6:00 A.M., drive by the Wrigley box office and buy
game day seats, then park downtown, have a pizza ahead of the
noon rush at Gino's, and take the "El" train up to Addison Street
in plenty of time for the game.

With Don, the difference was that we'd hold off on Gino's
until dinner, taking advantage instead of the lavish press lunch he
was sure Cubs management would provide. I trusted him to know
and believed when he said he gained ten pounds every fall covering Big Ten football, the free food was so good. "Great brats!" he'd
rave when I asked him what the press lounge at Kinnick Stadium
had to offer; he suspected Wrigley Field's facilities would boast
even more.

Don, a small-town Missouri kid whose job with the Waterloo
Courier had him living in the biggest city yet, was impressed by

how well I knew the Chicago traffic and how easily I got us parked and on the elevated train to Wrigley. We both panicked when it sped right past Addison Street, but I remembered that the El stopped here only from an hour before game time to an hour after the park closed up.

"We can walk the blocks from Irving Park Boulevard," I assured him, and as it happened we enjoyed this more leisurely approach that allowed the ballpark's physical structure to emerge so dramatically from the surrounding neighborhood brownstones. We were halfway down Clark Street and turning an angled corner before we saw it. But what a sight it was, like a black-and-white photo from the 1930s amid the city's dull bricks and sooty sidewalks. In a neighborhood of three-story apartment houses, it loomed monumentally; walking down these city streets and suddenly coming upon a battleship would not have been more impressive. Superstructure and all, even to the point of being decked out with pennants, Wrigley Field seemed as tightly parked into the square blocks bounded by Sheffield, Waveland, Clark, and Addison as would the USS *Missouri* nestled into dry dock.

The press gate was just one more turnstile, where instead of a ticket a kid asked to see a photo ID, then flipped through a stack of passes before finding ones with our names. It looked like a laundry tag, string and all, so I tied it to the shoulder strap on my jacket.

"That's how the Europeans do it," Don kidded. "Everyone'll think you're covering the game for *L'Express* or the Vatican newspaper!" But the knot was tied and I left it, never getting an odd look all day.

Far from it. The little tag was my credential in the best sense of the word, and I didn't even have to wonder if it deserved my confidence. From my first steps so empowered, I felt like I was walking on air. Moving through the damp gloominess of the not-yet-opened concessions stands beneath, we turned up a narrow rampway and stepped out into the sudden beauty of Wrigley Field. Having seen it so often on TV these last years, it was like appearing on the program itself. But the press pass meant something more, something reaching back to my earliest yearnings inside such parks. Not even waiting to see if Don followed—not willing to let his professionalism about some procedure to interfere—I strode purposefully down the aisle through tiers of field and club boxes.

An usher was at the field gate, and as I smiled hello he swung it open. Thanking him, I took the last half step through the opening in the low brick wall and down onto the gravel track. It crunched in a sensation of utter physicality I'd never felt before, the presence of a distant, fully different world suddenly pressing back, then yielding to let me in. Emily Dickinson writes of death this way, as do Japanese poets—about the split second at dawn where into the first sliver of light at the earth's horizon the hero can leap and thus enter eternity. For whatever baseball can be worth in the ultimate meaning of things, I felt I had done something at least a little bit like that.

Although it was early and there weren't many others in the park, I immediately felt apart from them. They were on the other side and I was down here, in the company not of ticket-holding fans but with Ryne Sandberg, Leon Durham, Jody Davis, and the others who from the other side of that line might as well have been on TV, for all you could reach them. Here you were among them, walking on the same grass that was theirs alone. For a while, the rules of baseball allowed them to share it with the likes of Don and me.

There were actually some other press people around. As this was the Giants' first trip into Chicago this year, the local media was out to get a look at newcomers like Will Clark and Robby Thompson. Plus the San Francisco writers, rather than lingering in the press lounge, were collecting information on the Cubs. This was good and kept me and Don from being spotted out as interlopers with nothing real to do. Even then it was pretty obvious the way I hovered near the batting cage when Billy Williams was there to coach a hitter or seemed so awestruck when the starting lineup's turn came for their swings.

The awe was reasoned and directed: Sandberg and Davis

seemed so much taller here than on TV, taller in fact than average people. It was the spikes, Don later told me, giving these guys an extra inch. But their height contributed to an enhanced sense of presence, these players looking so familiar yet so depthfully dimensional that I felt aswim in a hyperspace of virtualized reality.

Another fact made being down on the field among these players something other than real: that they were all going about their business completely oblivious to me and the other media around. True, Steve Stone from WGN might be sharing words with Giants manager Roger Craig while Cubs counterpart Jim Frey was deep in studied conversation with a newspaper reporter on the bull pen bench. But the players themselves took turns swinging and chatted with each other as if Don and I weren't there. Sandberg, Davis, Keith Moreland, and the others, without being offensive, looked right through us as they went about their work in this space we all shared. They might as well have walked right through us as well, for the eerie feeling I had just then was that I might indeed be a ghost.

In time the spookiness of being around the cage prompted me to wander off. Maybe there wasn't life after television, I reasoned—you could step across the line easily enough, but no way could you bodily enter that fourth dimension of the baseball world without becoming a player yourself. But Wrigley Field—and its bricks and grass, its gently curving stands and nicely wrapped ivy walls—was a hard and fast reality by itself, something I could stub my toe against, if I wished. And so I ambled down the left field line, keeping an eye out for batting practice fouls, to get a firsthand look at the climbing vines Bill Veeck had planted half a century ago.

"Hey buddy, don't take my picture!" With my camera's viewfinder focused on a close-up of the ivy, I hadn't noticed pitcher Steve Trout out there shagging flies. Startled to attention, I saw why he complained: There he was, fly open and uniform pants halfway down, adjusting his undershorts beneath a protective plastic cup.

"That's all I need," he laughed when seeing my surprise.

"You could sell it to *The National Enquirer.*" He had something of a screwball's reputation and probably had to worry quite seriously about photographers catching him looking stupid. Of course, maybe there was a better place to fix your plastic jock than at the left field foul line in Wrigley Field.

"No, no," I assured him, I was just getting some close-ups of the foliage—the wall's, not his. But that seemed to worry him all the more.

"Hey," he challenged, looking serious. "Who are you taking pictures for?"

"I'm from the Midwest League," I stammered, looking for a level of affiliation a bit more impressive than the Waterloo Indians.

"The Midwest League?" he cross-examined me. "There's a magazine called *The Midwest League?*"

"No, no," I repeated again. "I'm involved with a team in the Midwest League, Waterloo."

This gave Steve pause, and I wondered what was next as his expression showed great puzzlement.

"The Midwest League, the Midwest League . . . " he muttered, as if pondering a theorem of arcane Egyptology. Then, before I could help, he brightened.

"The Midwest League!" he stated with assurance. "I used to pitch in the Midwest League!"

Well, this was after all the son of Dizzy Trout, and I smiled along with him at his grand deduction. He then volunteered to pose for a picture—"waist up," because through all of this, his pants remained undone—and I snapped the shot, happy to share his private joke.

Back toward the Cubs dugout a minor commotion was taking place, so I trotted over for a look. There had been icons on the field already, such as publicist Ned Colletti and announcer Steve Stone, the latter with his trademark cigar looking here like a stage prop. He was going on with Giants coach Bob Lillis about how Hall of Famer Joe Morgan confided that Lillis had taught him how to play second base. Steve's eager, earnest singsong sounded just like on TV, and I wondered how Lillis could trust it. Two guys

who didn't sound like their he-man images were Keith Moreland
and rookie Will Clark, both of whom were complaining in high
squeaky voices to a Louisville Slugger rep that too much of the
lumber had been shattering lately. But the fuss at the dugout
turned out to be right in character, for here was Harry Caray,
making his first appearance of the day.

You couldn't miss him making his way down through the
stands like an ocean liner coming into berth. He moved as a creature of great displacement and seemed even more monumental
in the way he pressed through his adoring public, giving them
the same little smile and mechanical wave that suits the Queen
Mother on parade. Coming through the field gate and into the
Cubs dugout, he struggled with his pre-stroke girth and massive
belly, looking for all the world like a man lugging a twenty-seven
inch TV set. But to the players and press people saying hello, he
was all good cheer.

"Hi ya, fellas!" he beamed. "I gotta find Jim Frey for my radio
show. Anybody seen him?"

Heading back to the batting cage, where the Giants were out
for their session, I found Don Kruse hungry for lunch and eager
to show me how reporters like himself were cared for. At the top
of the stands we found a guarded door with the word "Offices" on
it, showed our passes, and were welcomed back to a set of rooms
overlooking Clark Street. The windows are visible in any of the
classic corner-of-Clark-and-Addison photos of the ballpark. Behind them are the club's offices down one side and press facilities along the other. The former looked as plush as any executive
suite—deep carpets, paneling, subdued lights—and I could picture Dallas Green back there in the deep recesses of power argu-
ing contracts and making trades. The press lounge was simpler,
all fluorescence and Formica, and from the adjustable minor league
rosters on one wall I guessed it served as a meeting room for the
farm system scouts and director. One approached a small table on
which sandwiches and bowls of thick soup were being offered—
cafeteria-style. A Pepsi tap at the side let you draw your own. Not

very fancy, but being for free, who could argue? The food itself was good. As Don promised, the brats were terrific.

Getting some food and our first rest of the day picked us up, and realizing that gametime was near we set out for the press box. From television broadcasts we knew right where it was, a narrow two-tiered affair suspended as a mezzanine beneath the first row of upper deck seating, wrapping around behind the plate roughly from dugout to dugout. A catwalk suspended above the grandstand took you there. But how to reach it?

With Wayne Messmer already singing the national anthem, we didn't have much time, so we began trying doors. All were locked except one standing an inch ajar, guarded by a security woman. "Press box," we chorused, flashing our credentials and moving past her amused stare. Pulling the door open, I could see what was so funny: It wasn't the stairwell to the catwalk after all but rather a storeroom for concessions.

"We're here to interview the hotdog buns!" I explained, then reversed course as Don started telling her about the great brats he'd had for lunch. The woman did point us to a ramp farther on, and taking it brought us to our destination. Although our assigned seats were at a table sitting out there on an exposed walkway to the right—auxiliary seating for the football press, Don explained, from when the Bears used to play here—the press box proper looked far from full, so we let ourselves in and sat down at the back.

That was no small thrill. In front of us sat the Chicago press corps, writers from the Bay area, and wire service reps, all equipped with laptops and phone lines to send their stories around the world. Down the line from us a short-order cook was flipping the greatest burgers imaginable from a grill awash with sizzling onions. I wanted one inordinately and took Don's advice to just ask. Fortunately, another writer was ahead of me, and I could see leaving a dollar tip seemed customary.

Soon the game was underway, and from here we watched the first inning. But it was turning out to be a beautiful day; the park was two-thirds empty, and the ancient press box with its heavy wood and mullioned windows was keeping us too much away from the good stuff. So with a nod to the cook we excused ourselves and went hunting for free seats below.

We found some in the club boxes just above the visitors' on-deck circle. This was sacred, longtime season ticket holder country, and we had hardly settled down before a very serious usher asked us to move.

I was ready to comply but soon learned what a genius Don Kruse was. He started putting out a line, dropping names from the Cubs' public relations staff—director Ned Colletti and assistant Sharon Pannozzo—and assuring the young man that if the ticket holders showed up we would clear out in a hurry. The usher still wanted us to move but didn't wish to force the issue and after a while gave up and left.

"How could those names impress him?" I challenged Don, expecting the usher to return with some beefy security types and hustle us out. "Anyone who watches Harry Caray hears them every day!"

"That wasn't it," Don explained. "Didn't you see who I was looking at, all the time I was talking?"

"I thought you were keeping an eye on the game," I said, but followed his gesture. A few rows down in front were two young black guys, whose boppy dress alone made them stand apart from the middle-aged fat cats and matron types typifying this part of the park.

"Those are his friends," Don informed me. "They don't have any business being down there. I was making it clear that I knew he'd let them in and that he'd better not complain about us." Don was right: The usher was a young African-American and didn't need a scene to show things up.

The game was pleasant enough, including the excitement of a couple Cub rallies that made it a thirteen-inning contest. It finally wound up when Candy Maldonado's home run went unanswered. As the game ended, a press conference of sorts developed out in front of the visitors' dugout, with Maldonado surrounded by reporters asking how he did it. We walked down through the field gate and joined the crowd, Don mumbling about how Candy, once a prospect in the Dodger farm system, had played in Iowa.

"Hey Candy," Don threatened to ask, "how is this different from Clinton?" Remembering Steve Trout's brain cramp over the Midwest League, I cautioned Don to leave the subject alone.

After the press crowd broke up, we followed the tunnel back from the dugout up a narrow catwalk into the visitors' clubhouse beneath the stands. It looked old, even quaintly institutional, its dull greens and browns reminding me of the bargain basement at Schuster's department store in Milwaukee nearly half a century ago.

Here Don intercepted the Giants' starting pitcher, Scott Garrelts, and pumped him with serious questions about, of all things, his hometown in downstate Illinois. Don knew the guy's high school from state tournaments, even the coaches' names in several sports. As he took notes—why, I wondered—his subject stood there politely, trained as athletes are for relating well to the media but surely wondering why he was doing this interview.

Once Garrelts had enough and politely excused himself, we retraced our steps, crossed the field, and made our way to the Cubs' locker room. Home team quarters had been recently rebuilt, and the difference was stunning. No Schuster's basement here. Instead, the place looked like the lobby of an upscale motel, nice carpet, stained redwood, and Naugahyde if not real leather. The lockers themselves were more like neat Williams-Sonoma shelving units, the only sign of tough-guy athletics being a single Bud Light beer can centered near the top in each, looking like a dashboard Jesus, a prayer for better days.

Because of the extra-inning loss, the mood was subdued. Here the only crowd was around Bob Dernier, who was patiently explaining that there was nothing special about his botched suicide squeeze; it was just a broken play. From time to time outfielder Gary Matthews, "Sarge" to TV viewers, would wander by, inappropriately chain-smoking away at a never-ending string of cigarettes.

Finally, as the room was beginning to clear out, we intercepted pitcher Rick Sutcliffe ("the Red Baron," in Harry's parlance) on his way to the showers. Buck naked, he didn't mind pausing for questions. Like his public image, he seemed the nicest guy around. Wondering where to look, I stood there for ten or fifteen minutes while Don drew him out on how his estranged father raced sprint cars at Knoxville, Iowa, and how Rick still returned there for pheasant hunting in the fall.

When Don started naming farms, wetlands, and hunting grounds, Sutcliffe visibly backed off.

"I have to be really careful about who I hunt with," he demurred, and for the first time we had to remember we were talking with a superstar earning several million dollars a year. His health and physical safety were his livelihood. Meanwhile my eyes had gone roving where they shouldn't, which surprised me even more than Sarge's nicotine Jones: Rick was pretty flabby around the middle, his gut in worse shape than my own. I suspected his Bud Light can was empty.

Thanking Sutcliffe for his time, we tunneled back to the dugout and out onto the field. Remembering how great the angle was from out in Steve Trout's shagger territory, I started heading once again down the left field line—only to be stopped by a polite young security guy who made it clear that the show and our attendant privileges were over. The field was off-limits now. In fact, the park would be closing up soon. I could get the shot I wanted tomorrow, he assured me and even recommended a specific millimeter lens.

Little did he know that this was it for me, that in a minute I'd step back over the line and perhaps never cross it again. It did feel sad pressing through the field gate back into the stands, becoming just one more fan with my memories.

Leaving Wrigley, we saw players in the guarded parking lot besieged by autograph seekers, only the less popular figures taking extra time to comply. At the back corner of Waveland and Sheffield Avenues, in the shadow of the park's massive hand-operated scoreboard, we saw the sidewalk overflowing with beer drinkers from Murphy's Bleachers. Even after training back to the Loop, we'd be spotted by folks who saw our scorecards and would ask how the Cubs had done.

"Yes," a businessman sympathized when hearing how the Cubs' closer, "Lee 'Lets-Make-It-Interesting' Smith," had blown the game. He knew we couldn't be that unhappy, for we'd had the beauty of an afternoon at Wrigley Field, a Renaissance museum of baseball, the Florence of the major leagues.

I used that line in the story I dutifully wrote for Don's paper. The piece was reprinted in one of Richard Grossinger's anthologies, and the phrase itself got excerpted in another book of baseball writing. So I had merited my press credentials after all, though I knew quite well the Cubs had given them simply as a show of good relations.

Don Kruse and I did the press pass routine once more, largely because he wanted to see a Brewer game. For me it meant getting an inside view of the County Stadium of my Milwaukee Braves youth. For an extra treat we decided to take in a White Sox game at Comiskey Park, still old Comiskey, doing a Brewer night game, sleeping at my mother's home, catching as much as we could of the next day's matinee, and then highballing down to Chicago's South Side for the other major league ballpark of my childhood. Milwaukee was playing Oakland, hot this year with two youngsters named McGwire and Canseco. The Sox were facing Cleveland, a natural enough attraction given our affiliation in Waterloo.

I'd warned Don how goofy cheesehead country could be, and he got a good dose of it right outside Milwaukee, where he wanted to grab some coffee.

"Hales Corners," he read off the village limits sign, "that sounds nice enough. And there's a Hardee's! How can we go wrong there?"

"Just wait," I assured him and was proven right by the folks in line ahead of us, a late-middle-aged couple in matching plaid wool jackets, who first asked the order person "What d'ya have?" and when directed to the menu display wanted to know the special of the day and whether the roast beef sandwich was end or center cut? When they handed over coupons for a breakfast muffin and didn't understand it was no longer being served I moved us to another line. Don got his coffee and admitted that he'd learned his lesson.

"Will the ballpark be like this?" he asked.

"Just wait," I promised him again, and this time he knew I meant it. Not that cheeseheadedness is all bad. Don liked it that the ushers checking our press passes acted like his grandfather back in Hermann, Missouri—"They think they're everyone's grandfather," I told him. And up in the press box, where the cold evening kept us, it was as folksy as the gang covering any minor league game. "Bek bek bek bek *bek*," the writers would all cluck, as a long drive sent an outfielder pedaling toward the fence. From time to time Bud Selig would wander over from his owner's suite next door, joking when his team was doing well, kicking the wastebasket when they weren't. The press lounge was a lot like Wrigley, the on-site food even better.

"Great brats!" Don kept mumbling through his food, a litany of brats, Polish sausage, smoked Italian links, and what all. Afterwards it was no problem standing around the visitors' locker room while players put away the postgame spread. I'll never forget how Reggie Jackson, his ample midriff spilling out of plenty-large undershorts, took a huge slice of pizza, folded it over into a sandwich, and snarfed away. Tony LaRussa, meanwhile, made his comments to the media sound like a law school seminar. Again, the facilities were anything but plush, this time reminding me of the boiler room and storage quarters back at Valley View School where our Cub Scout troop met.

Next day I insisted we get there early, and with Don waiting back in the press lounge for the Polish sausage to be readied, I walked down to the field. Even the earliest BP hitters weren't out yet, and I was the only person there.

Wanting nothing more than to take some interior shots of the visitors' dugout, I suddenly found myself sharing space with Ron Cey, out from the clubhouse to grab some fresh air. With no hesitation whatsoever, he started chatting with me—none of this treating the media like ghosts while doing pregame preparation as I'd noted at Wrigley. Well, he wasn't working now, I guessed, just someone looking for a pleasant chat in the warm noon sun after a frigid night game.

Was this his first trip to the ballpark in Milwaukee, I asked this veteran National Leaguer. No, as a Dodger he'd played an All-Star game here in the decade before. This time he found the park in much better shape, he confided, taking me for a local writer.

I asked him how he felt about shifting over to first base after a career at third. He said it was much easier than he'd thought, that he should have done it earlier as a way of extending his career. I asked if the fouls came differently, he said no—learning the position was mostly getting used to holding runners on.

All in all, it was a pretty normal conversation. Maybe here, back home, where in fact I felt most thrilled of all to be looking up at the stands from a position out on the grass, I had made a successful 100 percent crossing of the line. At least I looked sufficiently comfortable for Ron Cey, "the Penguin," to be at ease. I thought back to that Cubs locker room the year before and how amid the surprise of Gary Matthews's chain smoking and Rick Sutcliffe's beer gut he really did look like a penguin, even in street clothes. Well, I'd just passed part of the day with him and felt quite good about it.

"Nice talking with you," I said in parting. "Nice talking with *you*," Cey replied, and I think he meant it.

By now some players were at the cage, and a little scene developed in which some Brewer people mistook me for Sandy Alderson, the A's GM. When I told my son about it later, how the Brewers' counterpart Harry Dalton was also down there at the cage, he asked me why I didn't trade Reggie Jackson for Robin Yount. Very funny. But the staff's confusion was another credit for how natural I was looking here in baseball's own dimension.

It hurt to leave early, as Teddy Higuera was pitching a no-hitter in the fifth. But Don convinced me he didn't have good enough stuff to go all the way, and I was anxious to get to Comiskey Park early. We arrived in plenty of time, even as Bob Uecker's radio voice told us how Higuera was being knocked out of the box, and the only disappointment was seeing Comiskey standing there forlorn among expressway lanes and clear-cut urban renewal rather than emerging from the cozy neighorhood of shops and bars as it had in my youth. By now, my fourth time out, I felt confident enough about crossing the line that I could walk right through the scores of autograph seekers at the field gate, the usher letting me in by virtue of my manner alone.

After all the pregame stuff at the cage and in the locker room and following a quick food raid on the press box ("Great brats!"), Don and I took advantage of a strip of tickets from my ex-wife's law firm. Like princes, we had a full eight-seat box, right over the Sox on-deck circle, all to ourselves. On the whole, I decided, this was where I wanted to be. Don liked it too—it "wasn't like work," as he said, even though we had to pay for our subsequent food.

There was one more press pass to be had, however. Later that summer, to celebrate my son's high school graduation, I used what Don Kruse had taught me to secure credentials for Jonathan and myself to Fenway Park in Boston. It was a weekend series with the Mariners, doormat of the American League in those days, but that hardly mattered. Even before starting his journalism degree, Jonathan was being set up in a part-time sportswriting job at the Iowa City newspaper, thanks to a friend Don Kruse had there. But as for the kid crossing over the line, it would be me showing him the ropes.

Everything about the old park and its environs made for one of the nicest approaches ever: arriving by subway, or even walking from the old Copley as we did two days out of three; having the best baseball food yet, sweet Italian sausage sandwiches smothered in sautéed onions and peppers, vended off pushcarts in front of the stadium. Best of all was the ballpark itself, everything about it reduced in scale, from the narrow concourse underneath to the gentle rake—*easy sweep* is a better phrase for it—of the grandstand. No upper deck to speak of, though the press facilities were up on the roof, including a magnificent dining room and a bar, all mirrors and polished oak, that covered an entire wall.

No brats here: The Red Sox served us four course meals, with choices galore. And great company: Just one table over sat General Manager Lou Gorman with a pair of gray-haired, beet-faced monsignors, each of them looking more like Spencer Tracy than the other. Everyone on the staff was either Irish or Italian, and the whole scene seemed taken from an Edwin O'Connor novel.

On field, it was the same thrill as at Wrigley, Comiskey, or County Stadium, though Jim Rice and Wade Boggs were even stranger in their eerie self-isolation. The most fun came in prowling through the dugouts, tunnels, and locker rooms, all of which were truly ancient. Over the dugout telephone we found a list of inside numbers, and while I tried memorizing the digits for the bull pen Jonathan noticed a number with the words "pitching mound" next to it.

"No wonder Oil Can Boyd's so crazy," he laughed. "He's nuts because he can't find the phone out there!"

With Seattle not drawing much media attention, we had the place to ourselves, free to wander beneath the Green Monster and examine the little chicken shack inside the old scoreboard. My grandparents' basement, that's what it all reminded me of, everything quaint and dusty and incredibly *old*.

The slim presence of press corps during this dog days series with a weak, uninteresting team allowed several openings. On Sunday morning we arrived extra early, and when it turned out neither team was taking BP, the empty hours made the park our own. While Jonathan wandered its nooks and crannies, I played with photo angles from the visitors' dugout, the only person there until some shuffling cleats in the tunnel sounded the presence of Mariners coach Ozzie Virgil.

As old a baseball hand as they come, he had nothing else to do this fine Sunday morning other than hang around the field. It was a repeat of my experience at Milwaukee with Ron Cey—the guy just wanted to have some company in the quiet of this lovely ballpark before players and fans arrived and the whole hullabaloo began.

To my great surprise, our conversation became one of substance. After discussing all the weaknesses of this year's Mariners team—"We're short," Virgil kept saying as an explanation for it all—he asked me about our own operation back in Waterloo. Seattle was affiliated with the Wausau franchise, and when he mentioned that his organization was not terrifically happy there, I volunteered that Cleveland might be leaving us.

At this, Ozzie Virgil perked up, working me with very specific questions about what we had to offer. There was no doubt but that he was serious, and for once I felt I was accomplishing something valid here on this other side of the line, sitting on the dugout bench with one of the few dozen people in professional baseball who actually decide things about places like Waterloo. He thanked me for the information, giving every impression that something of substance would follow. I certainly hoped so, as our future with the Cleveland Indians looked bleak indeed.

Oddly enough, a similar conversation took place a couple of hours later. The July heat had sent us to the press box, where air conditioning didn't detract from our close view of the field. There were three rows, and we took seats in back—after three days, what had come to be our customary places. Next to us all weekend were two venerable people: Johnny Pesky, who as an extra coach had to be out of uniform and off the field by game time, and Carol Yawkey—*Mrs.* Yawkey, as everyone called her—widow of the club's legendary owner and still part of the directorship herself. By now, Pesky had become friendly enough to ask me about the minors, and when he found out I was from Waterloo, he got interested indeed.

"We used to have a club in Waterloo," he reminisced with a smile. "I coached there in 1968 and really enjoyed it!"

"You had Fisk," I mentioned, but he went right back to Waterloo in general and what a good time he had there.

"You know," he confided, drawing Mrs. Yawkey into the

discussion, "I'd really like to work in the minors again. . . . I think I could do a pretty good job managing at that level."

He then went on about how the Red Sox would be adding another A club and asked if there were any openings in the Midwest League. I could hardly contain myself as I ran through everything I'd told Ozzie Virgil and more. Good Lord—rather than being left high and dry by Cleveland, we could now be making a choice. And what a fantastic choice a Red Sox farm team managed by Johnny Pesky, so enthusiastic for Waterloo, would be!

Going back across the line from Fenway was no problem this time, no regrets at all. Instead I felt like I was sailing home with baseball's unique dimension in me. I was bearing inside news; I was truly a part of operating baseball, not just selling season tickets and helping out at the beer bar. I'd left Iowa as just one more venturer but was returning home a prophet.

And what is it that's said about a prophet in his own land? Oh, people were willing to hear my stories about how neat Fenway was, and they actually had questions about the park's more colorful eccentricities—about the Green Monster's surface, for example, and how its metal panels showed dents from every ball hit off it. But as for what Ozzie Virgil and Johnny Pesky had to say, that was nonsense. Just me talking through my hat. Or, at the very best, just those two guys doing the same. No way could I, just another board member, have access to such special news, much less be a figure in such dealings.

Okay, I thought, don't believe me—maybe I imagined it after all. One thing I did know was that when you cross the line back from baseball's special dimension, you can't bring it with you. The two worlds are discreet, and the only way deals do get done is because folks like Ozzie Virgil and Johnny Pesky and Lou Gorman up there with his monsignors in the Red Sox dining room carry it with them wherever they go. People like me, who only on rare occasions and then with somewhat bogus credentials get out on the grass, leave baseball's magic down there when we cross back over to the outside world.

What I'd experienced might as well have been fantasy, for its

realistic components were not portable to where we lived in
Waterloo. That affiliations did change hardly proved me right, for
it all happened so far above our own heads as to be transpiring
in the stratosphere. The Mariners pulled out of Wausau and put
their team in the Carolinas. On the thirtieth of September, at ten
minutes to five no less, on the last day legally possible for such
notification, Cleveland let us know the Indians would no longer
be affiliated with Waterloo. Having missed the chance at getting
Seattle, I reminded the board of Johnny Pesky's dream to manage
in our town, but my news was no more believable now. "Just talk"
was how my colleagues dismissed it.

     As it happened, the Red Sox added another A level team the
next year, placing it in the inferior South Atlantic League. Could
my contact with the old Rex Sox coach, remembered for holding
the ball in the 1946 World Series while Enos Slaughter scored
from first, have got them here? Seven years later they did join the
Midwest League; but by then Waterloo was out of baseball.

     They would have come only if my contact had been one of
many, part of a long series of exchanges around batting cages for
years and years. Sitting between them in Boston's press box, I
could marvel at the world Johnny Pesky and Mrs. Yawkey shared:
half a century of Red Sox business and plenty of nonbusiness,
too, such as fishing trips and hunting lodge days, when there was
a Mr. Yawkey as well. To the Yawkeys, Johnny Pesky was a fully
dimensional human being, as warmly real and as rich with shared
experience as any of my own close friends. But all that life was
across the line. To me he was just a player famous from the 1946
Series. And viewing it from where I was, across not only the line
but through the fogged glass of so many, many years, it was an
object of fantasy more than of fact.

     The two, fact and fantasy, do not mix. Which is why the
invisible line between a ballpark's seats and the grass marks the
most decisive barrier in any aspect of the sport.

Diamonds in the Rough:
Three Tales of a
Ball Club's Death

THE Waterloo Diamonds were the last minor league team to play in Waterloo, Iowa, a small industrial city that had hosted professional baseball since 1904. In 1994, three weeks before Opening Day, a group of club directors from which I had just resigned saw control of the team transferred to new owners, who moved it to Springfield, Illinois. In one afternoon all the paraphernalia needed to run things was loaded into a rented truck that headed south from town, and—except for all the ill feelings—that was that.

Yet this ending was a long time coming, and since then the process has repeated itself in many longtime minor league venues across America. Waterloo, Bristol, Gastonia, Fresno, and dozens of other towns once had professional baseball, and none of them has it now. It's not a happy story.

Three narratives about our own franchise's death exist, and I have a part in each. The first, quite simply, is the public record as noted in newspaper accounts. The second is my novel *Basepaths*, published by Johns Hopkins University Press in 1995 but written in Ireland and England following the 1991 season, the time when our little world of baseball started going bad. The third is Richard Panek's *Waterloo Diamonds*, a profoundly literary piece of personal journalism whose planning dates back to 1991, just as I was drafting my book, and which was finally published by St. Martin's Press in June 1995, just a month after *Basepaths* appeared.

Although all are focused on the same event, these three narratives tell their stories in remarkably different ways. But not so differently as to disagree over essentials. Comparing them shows that no matter what the bias and genre for expressing it, there is deep agreement on the effect of this ball club's departure, the inescapable consequence of seeing a minor league baseball club so often idealized as an image of life's renewal go belly up and die. In Richard Panek's initial interest, as in the organization's stated purpose and my own earlier fictionalizing of it, there had been a shared, sincere belief: that when it came to mortal imperfections, baseball could somehow rise above them. The truth, however, is that in trying to codify this perfection all three accounts run squarely into idealism's nether side.

As a franchise, the Waterloo Diamonds were run by a group of people who never knew they were idealists until it was too late: when everything was over, leaving some of them cynical about everything back to the start. Once upon a time the team had been conventionally owned, back in the earlier decades of the century when minor league baseball was a thriving business. By the 1960s, however, the loss of its fan base to television and other diversions had transformed ownership into stewardship, with local business people and other chamber of commerce types passing the hat each spring for start-up money and serving as a board of directors to make sure the operation didn't get too close to broke before each season's end.

Capitalization wasn't an issue, as the major leagues supplied players and city government provided the stadium—in Waterloo's case, a ballpark built in 1946 with fan donations. The third factor, a franchise to compete in the Midwest League, was a matter of keeping current with dues. Selling tickets, advertising, popcorn, hot dogs, and beer covered that plus team travel and utility bills, salaries for the general manager and groundskeeper, and hourly wages for the high school kids who worked concessions. All told, about nine hundred thousand dollars came in each year and that same amount went out. If there was five or ten grand left at year's end, it went to fixing something in the stands or improving the field. A couple of times bills were still unpaid in fall after the cashflow had ceased, in which case the club borrowed what it needed until season tickets and program ads could be sold come spring.

Such was the ball club's status when I got involved in 1978. By then the snappy business people were drifting away and more humdrum folks taking over, another consequence of minor league baseball's lack of appeal. In the pre-television 1940s, Municipal Stadium would be packed each night. But by the 1970s those who didn't watch baseball on the tube went out and played it themselves. On most summer nights, one could climb to the top of our grandstand, look back to the big, brightly lit softball complex just beyond our parking lot, and see more folks playing or waiting to play than were taking in the game we had to offer. A stadium once routinely jammed beyond capacity with seven thousand fans now averaged nine hundred per home date. Take away the half dozen big nights when the John Deere factory brought out its employees or a foodstore promotion bought out the park, and you had plenty of games played before a hardcore group of just a couple hundred regulars.

But both the smaller fan base and the simpler board of directors made for a more cherished diamond in the rough. As major league baseball ended its own hiatus from popularity and began producing astronomically salaried, larger-than-life superstars such as Reggie Jackson and Carlton Fisk, we prided ourselves on offering a more intimate product. Even as Boston's famous backstop sulked his way from the Red Sox to Chicago, Waterloo baseball could tout itself as the place where a younger and more innocent Fisk had played his first professional game back in 1968. By the time new Comiskey Park opened, fans would have to pay inflated prices to sit far up beyond the sky boxes and luxury suites to see him and his teammates squander chances at one championship after another as they squabbled with White Sox ownership over even bigger financial shares. Yet if you'd been a Waterloo regular in 68, you could have chatted with Fisk before the game, driven him home afterwards, perhaps even rented him your own grownup kid's disused room. Earlier in the seventies you'd have seen almost all of what became the pennant-winning 1980 Kansas City Royals win their own Midwest League championship as twenty-year-olds—and paid just a few bucks a night for the privilege, first-row seats and all. At present we had a rather lackluster affiliation with the Cleveland Indians, but when their inevitable rebound came you could rightly claim to have seen Greg Swindell's first pro game and even to have known Albert Belle as a softspoken young man, polite to everyone who'd care to say hello.

In such circumstances our volunteer board of directors ran things through the 1980s. There were ups and downs, good teams and bad, a pair of league championships, and several personable managers and coaches: former big leaguers such as Steve Swisher, who'd raised hell with Pete Vuckovich and Kenny Reitz on the 1979 St. Louis Cardinals, and Chuck Stobbs, who on April 17, 1953, had served up a pitch at the old Washington Senators' Griffith Stadium that Mickey Mantle hit 565 feet, as baseball's first tape-measured home run. Although some of the top draft picks who passed through could be a bit distant, there were plenty of personable eighteen- to twenty-three-year-olds who knew quite well they'd never beat the one-against-twenty odds of advancing all the way to the majors. In a couple years they'd be working for IBM or teaching junior high phys ed, and these guys proved eminently approachable. From the start I was always there around the cage for batting practice, and once put my back out for a week shagging BP balls in the outfield. During games I'd sometimes leave my friends in Box 28 near the on-deck circle to spend a few innings sitting on the low wall next to our left field bull pen, chatting with the relievers and utility men but mostly taking in their game time conversations. Afterwards I'd help roll out the tarp and see what the groundskeeper had to say.

With the April-through-August minor league season advancing like a narrative, I felt like I was inside a living story. And so to extend the experience I began in 1979 drafting little vignettes covering the ongoing events of a fictional baseball club I called the Mason City Royals. Sometimes a story took off from what had happened with our real-life club, while usually I just made things up—but all as a way of filling my mornings with this style of baseball before mid-afternoon arrived and I could go out and find something happening at the park.

The result was *Short Season*, written between 1979 and 1985 and (after thirty-five commercial rejections) published by Johns Hopkins University Press in 1988. Though its twenty-eight stories follow the course of a single minor league season, it was written in bits and pieces, with no regard for chronology, until with a couple hundred pages of work completed I sorted things out and finished up by filling in some holes. The result was what postmodern theorists might call diachronic synchrony, a narrative dedicated to a simple five-month progression while in the process drawing on six years of real and imaginative experience, all of it thoroughly mixed up as composed.

For me, the motive for such a narrative was clear. Though other things were changing, baseball and my involvement in it remained the same. No matter what else, each April we'd have a season opener, and every late August the games would come to an end. Meanwhile I was writing *Short Season*, taking something from 1982 as it happened, something else from a memory of 1978 or '79, and even more from how I imagined things not yet happening might someday turn out. In the short run, I was sustaining my interest in the ball club when I couldn't be with it myself. As for larger dimensions, my manner of writing made it as timeless as possible, even as the basic building blocks were temporal units: individual games, three-game series, week-long home stands and road trips, all of it starting in April and ending with August. *Any* April, *any* August. Though my collection followed a year's assemblage of Mason City Royals through one competitive year, it could have been any year and every year, and was.

This same timelessness of traditional minor league baseball drew Richard Panek to Waterloo. A professional writer from New York, formerly on the staff of *Seven Days* and presently working on assignments for *Mirabella*, the New York *Times*, and other such outlets, Richard phoned me in fall of 1991. He'd read *Short Season*, liked it, and remembered its idea of a minor league summer when an editor suggested he write a nonfiction book on the subject. Richard's interest was sincere, motivated much like my own. He'd recalled how during the baseball strike of 1981 he and some college friends at Northwestern University's Medill School of Journalism were lamenting that they couldn't go as planned to see the Chicago Cubs and how they'd discovered minor league ball as a substitute. Left alone as they were, the minors were strike-free—and also cheap, intimate, and by virtue of being on a slower track, quite old-fashioned, more like Richard's childhood memories of the Cubs than the slickly promoted product temporarily out of service at Wrigley Field.

Yet sincere as Richard Panek was, his editor was probably looking past such idealism to a very real development just now taking place. After decades of neglect, minor league baseball was becoming popular. Not popular "again" in the sense of being a routine pastime for people in large towns and small cities but in the manner of becoming trendy among a clientele whose entertainment dollar is spent according to ever-changing fashion. With abundant cash and unlimited credit generated by the Reagan years, new types of owners entered the field: business people from New York, Chicago, and Los Angeles, who thought owning a ball club in the Midwest League could be both fun and profitable. Overnight, it seemed, the Kenosha Twins were being operated by a Manhattan sports psychologist consulting for CBS Television, the South Bend White Sox were acquired by a Hollywood producer of *The Bill Cosby Show*, and the Quad City franchise—

where Richard Panek had seen minor league ball much earlier in the decade—was one of five bought up around the country by a hotshot young developer who'd made a fortune turning derelict Chicago buildings into high-priced lofts and condos for gentrifying yuppies.

This last example typified baseball's new strategy. Like those run-down properties in Chicago, minor league franchises had been neglected so long that they could be acquired for little more than outstanding debts. Fixed up and marketed according to the whiz-bang techniques of this new business age, they could turn a decent profit by attracting a better salaried, larger spending crowd. Soon the franchises themselves would have some worth— at which point they'd be sold at inflated prices to still newer owners, who with the need to recover their investments cranked up marketing yet another notch. By the eighties' end small-time baseball was big stuff, big enough for movies. From the simplicity of W. P. Kinsella's Iowa cornfield become diamond in the rough for *Field of Dreams* to quaint old Durham Athletic Park in *Bull Durham*, America's entertainment industry got on the bandwagon, leaving us in Waterloo with a puzzling question: Where was this razzle-dazzle parade leaving us?

The sad answer was that it left us behind. When Richard Panek called, I had to tell him that our recently concluded season had not been a happy one. For the first time in a long time there'd been some significant changes, ones that affected the nature of minor league ball and about which I was now writing.

"A sequel to *Short Season*?" Richard asked, and I quickly explained the hundred-some pages I'd drafted and the impetus for writing them. The minors' new popularity had caught Major League Baseball's interest, especially since franchises that they themselves had abandoned as worthless a generation before were now changing hands at rapidly escalating prices: from ten thousand dollars not so long ago to in excess of one million this past year. Irritated at carrying so much expense in operating their farm systems in the face of such apparently selfish profit, big

league owners and executives had begun compelling their affiliates in the minors to comply with a new Professional Baseball
Agreement covering everything from vastly improved ballpark
conditions to the minors assuming a much greater share of costs.
Franchises with New York and Hollywood owners would have no
trouble meeting these demands. But folks like us, with no capital
to improve our substandard stadium and few skills for turning the
operation into a thriving business, were in poor shape. One by
one, mom-and-pop outfits like the Waterloo Diamonds—which,
as a new affiliate of the San Diego Padres, we were now called—
were being forced out. The Wisconsin Rapids franchise had been
declared defunct; Wausau, once owned by a local dairy farmer
and playing in a tiny bandbox of a stadium nestled in less than a
square block of town, had been purchased by some Chicago lawyers and moved to a glamorous new sports facility built for them
in wealthy suburban Kane County, Illinois. Other such franchises were in similar trouble, struggling like us to make the
changes necessary to survive. And, as I told Richard, it wasn't
much fun.

Yet fun was what I wanted to have. That's what had struck
me shortly after I started to write, once I'd gotten past my initial
disappointment with the 1991 season and a false start at simulat-
ing the old idealism. Getting far away from it all helped. For the
last decade and a half—coincidental with involvement with baseball, as it happened—my wife and I had begun each autumn by
spending a quiet month abroad. Lately that month spanning the
end of September and the start of October had been in Ireland
and England, with a couple weeks each in the wilds of North
Connemara and Dartmoor, where it was so peaceful and easy to
write. Here, with our usual room in Mallmore House on Clifden
Bay and sole proprietorship of the turf fire in a sitting room once
used by the Bishop of the West Indies (himself an ocean away
from his sinecure) and then Lady Baden-Powell, I fled the hassles
of our just concluded baseball year. Sitting down that first night,
jetlag and all, I wasn't even sure what I'd do. Something on World

War II air combat memoirs was a possibility, as was continuing with an account of working with contemporary fiction writers—both were projects underway at home that would benefit from some more writing over here. But the blank page called for baseball, and so in the hours before the fire died and Julie expected me to turn in I drafted a scene, as it were, from life: the description of an utterly fortuitous flight home from this same Ireland two years before, when the domestic leg from Boston to Chicago and then Waterloo had taken us over three major league ballparks and one minor league stadium, our own.

That flight had been on September 26, 1989—still happy days with the Waterloo Diamonds and a good year for cheering my favorite big league club of the moment, the Cubs. That year we'd taken off on August 30, right after our last home game, and were returning to the promise of playoff and World Series tickets via our San Diego connections. While changing planes in Boston, I bought a *USA Today* and learned the Cubs would probably clinch at Montreal that night. And so with baseball quite pleasantly on my mind, I settled back to enjoy another childhood thrill that has never gone stale: flying. Despite my fifty years and graying beard and millions of passenger miles, I always take the window seat and gaze raptly at everything along the way.

This late September night had been a spectacular one for flying. Crystal clear with no obscuring humidity or haze, the weather made some wonderful things possible, starting with an early dusk takeoff from Logan and a low turn that took us across the city just south of Beacon Hill, the Back Bay, and Fenway.

Yes: Fenway Park, awash in light for a Red Sox game against the Yankees. Bright as the old city was with tightly packed illumination, the ballpark stood out like a jewel on cloth, with all that immense candle power focused on the playing field so that even at night Wade Boggs could see the rotating seams on an eighty-mile-per-hour curveball. Our DC-10 was at about five thousand feet, and from that mile up I could see details quite clearly: not just the stands, the infield dirt, and the outfield's sward of green but tiny figures spotted here and there in center, left, and right, their white uniforms catching every bit of the park's great lights. Visitors at bat, I thought, and checked my watch to see that indeed the game was just starting.

As happens in the scene I described two years later and that with altered characterization and plot became the first chapter of *Basepaths*, I spent the next two-and-a-half hours staring down at the baseball world below. First at Fenway, whose bright point of light, starkly white against the city's enveloping yellows and greenish blues, stood out for an hour as we winged our way at altitude over New England and western New York State. The night was not only free of clouds but moonless as well, and even as the pilot said we were overflying Buffalo I could crane around, see a smudge of light so many hundred miles distant that I'd kept oriented since leaving, and be convinced that the pinpoint at its center was Fenway Park—where I guessed that Wade Boggs in his second time at bat was seeing the ball better now that dusk had passed into full night.

Then, as the plane shifted course to take us over Lake Erie, I gave up looking back toward Boston and began peering ahead. Nine times out of ten this flight would pass above Detroit, and I hoped I might see Tiger Stadium. Other trips had shown me the old ballpark in Cleveland and Cincinnati's Riverfront Stadium from similar heights in daytime, their geographic locations at water's edge making them as evident in clear weather as schematics on a map. Brilliant as things looked tonight, I trusted I could plot the Tigers' yard from six miles high, following John Cabot Lodge Expressway in to where it turned just before the Ambassador Bridge and passed the ballpark.

With *USA Today* telling me the team was home tonight (against Toronto), I watched the dome of light ahead slowly define itself into patterns. There was Windsor coming up first, then the much brighter mass of Detroit itself; that narrow ribbon of darkness in between was the Detroit River, spanned by a shiny sliver I knew was the bridge to the United States. In the few minutes I had while passing overhead I picked my route, and on the animated map beneath me traced an apparent inch to my left—and there was Tiger Stadium.

In what became *Basepaths*, I had my viewer distinguish infield brown from outfield green. I know that from thirty-six thousand feet it's not possible, but by this stage in the narrative my character wanted desperately to see such detail, just as I wanted to. What I saw was the piercing concentration of light that indicated Tiger Stadium's location in the larger grid pattern of downtown Detroit. Because the stadium's outside walls are painted white I could see the contrast formed with the central green, spotlighted as it was with so much concentrated power.

What did impress me as the truth is that with Boston scarcely out of sight I'd been able to pick up Detroit, and that in each town there was an American League ball game being played. In my lap were stats for each starting pitcher, but before my eyes were the living games themselves. Each run was on the other's scoreboard, and anywhere east of the Rockies someone with a good AM radio could switch from one play-by-play account to the other, much as I'd tuned my way around the majors as a kid forty years before. But tonight was special, for here I was: up in the sky, still en route from the other side of the world, overseeing a good part of tonight's action in the American League East. Maybe even more if we swung into Chicago from the south and descended over Comiskey Park, where *USA Today* said the Sox were playing . . .

Sitting there in Ireland, remembering the flight from two years before, I did what all fiction writers do: I made it better than life. In 1989 I hadn't seen Comiskey Park up close, just its light towers as we cruised down the lakefront and turned inland over the Loop. But in 1991 I let my perceiving character, so excited by connections from ballpark to ballpark and anxious to keep connected to professional baseball himself, glide right over old Comiskey low enough to see the players. Before my night ended, I'd see Waterloo Municipal Stadium, just as my character would catch a view of the mythical ballpark in Mason City on his connection's last stop before Minneapolis.

As I clarified for Richard Panek a month or so later, what I'd begun over in Ireland and England and was now finishing at home didn't continue in the blithesome spirit of my first baseball book or even of this first chapter of the next one written abroad. Instead, as I sat there in Connemara and then on Dartmoor, my new baseball narrative evolved into a different kind of story. Recent troubles had made me more concerned with management, on and off the field. This past season's hassles with the new Agreement had made those doings more problematic. And most problematic of all was that it was all related, just as what I could see happening at Fenway was related to the other parks I flew over that night two years before.

Richard's own plan was to come out next spring for Opening Day, stay a couple weeks, then come back for key home stands and road trips during the season, following the team for its competitive five-month "year" and picking up a feel for our franchise's operation along the way.

That would be too late, I cautioned him. Better to start right now, before fall turned into winter and the rules for next year's baseball would be set. The Midwest League was gathering in November, readying itself for the annual Winter Meetings with Major League Baseball scheduled for the first week in December. By the time winter itself set in, everything now still up in the air would be determined, with the baseball season itself simply left to play things out according to plan. Because of all the turmoil over the new Professional Baseball Agreement and how to implement it, the real action for ownership would be now—just as on more specific levels minor league general managers would be planning their promotions while farm directors figured out who'd coach and manage where.

And so as I finished *Basepaths* Richard Panek began, half a year earlier than intended, to follow league business and legal wranglings between the majors and the minors. By the time of his first visit—in March 1992, well ahead of our April opener—he'd schooled himself on the business side of baseball that I'd learned

over more than a decade by working my way up to the club's
executive board and finally being elected secretary.

By the time Richard began tapping prototypical sections of
Waterloo Diamonds into his ever-present laptop computer, I'd
taken the longhand manuscript of *Basepaths* and banged it out
on my IBM Selectric III. Friends in Box 28 read it, and I gave
Richard a copy as well, which he said he'd hold off reading until
season's end. Nevertheless, folks kept telling him how eerie it was
that so many of the things I'd presented as fiction were, as spring
and summer progressed, one by one coming true. True, but with
a difference: What happened in *Basepaths* was sarcastically funny,
while the fortunes of our ball club were sad indeed, as Richard
could see before him. By the time it was all over, there was a third
account as well, coming from the public business as reported by
the Waterloo *Courier*. What's interesting to see now that all three
versions are complete is how each begins with great hopes for
baseball and each ends with those hopes dashed, leaving a resi-
due of pessimism about the minors and how they're run. Only the
manner of dashing is different.

Basepaths charts a very simple, almost mechanical course
toward destruction, as two complementary operations get off to
shaky starts at opposite ends of the country. Because both involve
preparations for the same coming season, the necessity of their
eventual convergence makes disaster a foregone conclusion. My
rhapsody about flying home over those ballparks now served as a
rookie manager's introduction to this new level of the game. I
made the occasion his late-season return from a job hunting trip,
where he's been off interviewing for a coach's position in college
ball. Seeing all these big league ballparks and how they're linked
to the minors makes him opt for a managing job at Class A Mason
City, starting in the spring. The Kansas City Royals, with whom
he's just concluding his major league career, announce this as-
signment about the same time as the Mason City Royals' board of
directors make their own key hire, choosing an assistant general
manager from down South to take over duties as GM for their

franchise. Soon action is developing on two fronts: at minor league spring training in Florida, where Ken Boyenga and the other Royals farm club managers sort out their players, and in Iowa, where the Mason City folks prepare for the business end of their coming season.

To make the mix more volatile, rookies on both sides abound. Not only are Ken Boyenga and the new general manager, Jim Hunt, untested in their leadership roles, but plenty of those around them are new at it, too. As is customary in minor league development, where after a year players either go up a level or out, nearly all of Boyenga's roster slots are filled by guys new to Mason City. This year the local board of directors has some changes too, from a chronically malcontent electrician being elected president (so he can't complain, his colleagues hope) to the recruitment of a new member, garbage contractor Mike Jacobs, who promises to not let ignorance of tradition impede his self-serving activism.

Unlike *Short Season*, *Basepaths* was written chronologically, its development following the course of parallel lines that within the infinity of fiction finally intersect. After home and neighboring away openers the Mason City Royals travel across the state for their first long road trip, during which Lois Boyenga, the manager's wife, journeys from West Virginia to Iowa. Her plan is to surprise Ken with a newly set up home in Mason City, rented with the help of the oldest, nicest, and most altruistic member of the board, Lefty Dunsmoor, whose life runs a parallel but contrasting course with the shenanigans of avaricious Mike Jacobs. And even as Ken Boyenga moves forward in his new role of responsibility, the curse of his rowdy past shows up to bedevil him in the persons of two Pete Vuckovich-like and Kenny Reitz-like teammates. Scarcely a week into the season both baseball operations, on field and off, blow up right in their makers' faces, as the most preposterous features of each collide in a head-on smashup. While others pick up the pieces, Ken Boyenga is recalled to Kansas City for what's sure to be his dismissal. But on the way is another airplane flight, one that to the little boy sitting behind the chastened manager is quite spectacular, right over the minor league ballpark in Des Moines that had been Ken's last stop before making the majors. For now, it's just the last stadium he'll be seeing as a pro.

Basepath's first review, in *Publishers Weekly* (April 24, 1995), grasped exactly what these pratfall parallels and slapstick collisions were about: "Everyone in this flat Iowa landscape is minor-league himself, yet likable: the red-faced club president; his cheapskate garbage-collector colleague; a hairy redneck car salesman named Crazy Jim. In fact, the players and game are little more than a backdrop to the host of well-drawn middle-aged screwballs that train, fund and feed the teams out of dedication to the sport" (p. 62). The fact that many of my characters were indeed screwballs of the first order made the humor come easy, but their comic malfeasance alone was not the point. Nothing any of them did was indictable. That's why when everyone is brought together at the police station near the end, all charges are dropped: It's not a crime to be stupid, which is ultimately the worst one can say about club president Al Swenson, new member Mike Jacobs, ex-big-league fun lovers Jeff Copeland and Don Kruse, or even Mike Jacobs's partners in garbage and fast-buck memorabilia, Moose and Toad. None of them are geniuses, let alone evil geniuses. They're all just a bunch of clueless screwballs.

But look at what happens because of their screwiness: Baseball, on field and off, is destroyed, with innocent people taking the blame. It's the most generously good person in the whole narrative, Lefty Dunsmoor, who winds up bearing the brunt of Kansas City's rage. And Ken Boyenga, whose only culpability was once having goofy friends and who has been doing a good job running his new team, is the single person canned. While those who have made a fetish of baseball wander off to their next delusion, it's the purists who are left to suffer.

A different structure and broader thematics inform Richard Panek's *Waterloo Diamonds*. After brief introductions to on-field and off-field operations, *Basepaths* had let its story be told in just the first ten days of play, days in which everything so carefully prepared is deconstructed as only a group of French literary theorists or middle-aged screwballs could manage. Richard's book not only covers the entire 1992 season in Waterloo but also carries on through the off-season struggles and nightmares of 1993, ending with the franchise's collapse in March 1994. In the process, matters of social history, politics, geography, demographics, and economics are examined in their present manifestations and researched more than a century back for deeper understanding. Yet the author puts his major focus on several key personalities involved, and as these people get caught up in larger forces of business and government *Waterloo Diamonds* begins reading a little bit like *Basepaths*, screwballs and all.

Personality conflicts have a lot to do with Richard's narrative. At greatest reach, it's the difference between the powerful heights of the majors and the lowly weakness of the minors, true for both business and athletic aspects. Within the minors, there's the contrast between new-style successful franchises and old-time struggling ones like our own. In Waterloo itself, there's conflict between city government and the board of directors, between the well-off community activists and the much shabbier baseball crowd. In the club's front office, general manager Dave Simpson's austere bottom-line approach is challenged by assistant GM Jeff Nelson's more exuberant, sometimes reckless style of marketing and promotion. And so on, all the way to different motives everyone has for being involved with the game.

It's by means of such contrast and conflict that I'm introduced, set off against my friend Jeff Copeland's milder manner (it was with rich irony that I'd named the rowdiest character in *Basepaths* after him). Jeff and I are posed as opposites when it comes to facing the prospect of having to sell out if we couldn't meet the new Professional Baseball Agreement standards:

> One owner in particular had become especially vocal in his criticism of Simpson. Jeff Copeland and Jerry Klinkowitz were professionally and

personally close. Both were professors of English at the University of Northern Iowa, and it had been at Klinkowitz's suggestion, in fact, that Copeland joined the board. Temperamentally, however, they were opposites. Copeland, round-faced, soft-spoken, was an accommodationist, a perpetual seeker of the middle ground. During a board discussion of Simpson's idea of charging fees to other users of the ball field, Copeland tried to quell tempers by suggesting that the owners form a community relations committee. Klinkowitz, by contrast, was an absolutist. He never gave ground, and he never gave up. Spread-eagling his arms at a board meeting, jackaloping up the grandstand steps during a game, Jerry Klinkowitz would press his point while pursuing his prey—who, as often as not these days, was Simpson. At that same discussion of fees, Klinkowitz waved an open palm toward Simpson and invoked the name of the owner of the Quad City franchise: "This man would be the best GM for Rick Holtzman. His bottom line is money. That's not our bottom line. Our bottom line is to keep baseball here as long as possible."

"But that takes money!" an incredulous Simpson answered him. "We've gotta meet major league statutes!"

"We've got to be sharing! Altruistic!"

"We made money last year."

"We made enemies, too. And just at the time we can least afford it."

"I thought," Simpson said, shaking his head, "you-all *wanted* me to make money for you."

"*We* don't make any money off this!"

To which Simpson replied, wearily, "Yeah, you do. You get a million. You split it fifteen ways."

It was on this point that Klinkowitz's arguments with the GM always broke down. Klinkowitz, nearing fifty, was the son of a Milwaukee beer salesman, and though he'd left his beginnings behind through a long career in teaching and writing (among his published works was a collection of short stories about minor league ball, *Short Season*), he'd immediately identified in the ball club's directors, when he met them back in the 1970s, an assembly of like-minded souls. What his fellow owners took for granted, he exalted, and over the years he'd emerged as the board's most ardent defender of tradition by far. For Klinkowitz, selling the ball club wasn't an option. Technically, Dan Yates at the previous meeting had suggested only announcing that the ball club was for sale, in the hope of prompting emergency action from the city or flushing out a local investor or donor. For Klinkowitz, however, even *announcing* that the club was for sale wasn't an option. It wasn't even their *right*.

"We are not the owners," he'd said. "We are the stewards. We are in charge of keeping baseball here, and that's all. We knew it wasn't going to be easy, and now that it's not is no time to quit."

But, as Copeland and Yates pointed out, if the board members waited, they risked having nothing. The franchise might cease to exist; or it might revert to the Midwest League; or—who knew? The stadium renovation deadline of April 1, 1994, was going to come and go and all the owners might have to show for their noble intentions were fond memories and an empty ballpark.

"Fine," Klinkowitz said. "That's as it should be. That's how this club *should* fold—with us clawing in the dirt until the last dollar is gone." (pp. 132–133)

Thus I become the purist of Richard Panek's story, albeit in a rather screwball way. As time passes and our struggles increase, Richard shows how what was once my most dire Cassandra-like prophesying slowly becomes sordid fact, as powers in the community write off the team's directors as "a bunch of nobodies" and begin taking a hundred times more money than needed to save baseball and directing it toward an arcane urban national park project that would make a tourist monument of Waterloo's failed industrial/agricultural economy.

The pessimism in Richard Panek's account comes from the simple truth that with business success now mandatory, minor league baseball has passed Waterloo by. Purism no longer counts, with some doubt as to whether it ever did. In any event, it alone can no longer sustain an operation where the economic base is lacking.

Cautious not to sentimentalize, Richard clarifies just who suffers. Not a lot of people: just a few hundred hardcore fans, the regulars who didn't wait for a big promotion or free ticket to attend games. And not powerful or influential or even moderately well-off folks, either—just an aging, working class crowd whose interests didn't compute when it came to evaluating the connunity's interests. Yet Richard's book is one of literary journalism and not just reportage. A major part of his task is to make readers appreciate baseball's presence and sense its loss, and for this he coincides with *Basepaths* in making the very best person in his book suffer the most for all the ill doings of larger powers and smaller fools.

That person is Mildred Boyenga, club president during its better days and savior when problems first arose in the later 1980s. I chose her last name for my fictive manager as a tribute, and Richard uses her character as the focus for Waterloo baseball's joy, struggle, and demise. One of the last old-timers, she remembers how different the operation was a generation past, and in these present days she can responsibly lament the loss of ideals. In Richard's narrative she becomes allied with Iowa itself, a landscape introduced and referred to several times in terms of two simple human actions: how here at the prairie's edge one's gaze rises naturally to the broad sky while one's hands reach down to feel the richness of the soil. This is the general image with which *Waterloo Diamonds* begins, and it's repeated in various circumstances throughout, including one time when the league president leaves me and the club president standing hopeless in the outfield, an improvised conference on saving the team having come to naught. It also defines the specific moment Richard chooses for his story's end, staying with Mildred and her thoughts after the meeting—to begin selling the club—adjourns:

> Boyenga didn't budge. Some of the other owners were pulling up their chairs in a circle a few tables away, and she supposed she would join them soon, but for a moment she remained off to the side of the room, not moving from her chair. One morning, a beautiful morning, she had driven to Waterloo Memorial Park Cemetery, on the southwestern edge of town, and not far from the entrance had stopped at an unmarked stop under a tree. It had been a memorable autumn, slow and lingering, a gradual surrender of one season to the next. The trees in the cemetery blazed the color of pumpkins, plums, gourds, and figs. A breeze reached her. She turned to face the sun. Autumn in these parts could be so brief, hardly a pause at all between the two long hauls of summer harshness and winter fierceness. But this year fall was taking its time. She bent to the earth next to the tree. The dirt was still soft: no first frost yet. She rested her hand against the soil and surveyed the view from here: grass, the Veterans Memorial monument, the tree. It was an ideal spot, and she had to won-

der why it was still available. It occurred to her that it might have something to do with the roots of the tree, that their entangling, consum-
ing growth would lend whatever rested underground here a certain imper-
manence, but then she decided that she simply didn't want to think about
it, that she was, in fact, tired of thinking, and that she wouldn't al-
low her doubts to intrude upon and spoil such a perfect specimen of an
autumn day in Iowa: a gentle breeze, and whispering trees, and the open
sky.

She stood up. Mildred Boyenga brushed the dirt from her hands and,
for now, walked away from her grave. (pp. 372—373)

In real life—not in fiction or in image-rich literary journalism—Richard Panek had been with Mildred that day visiting the
cemetery, as he had spent many days with her learning about
Waterloo and its baseball from her point of view. As an artist,
however, he could guess where her mind was as this meeting
ended, and I pulled up a chair with some others on the board to
issue more dire warnings about how grim the future could be.

And grim it was. Realizing we could never maintain the operation ourselves, we sought help to keep minor league baseball
here—and ran into opposition from almost every conceivable direction. Newspaper coverage was extensive, informing the public
about what we'd learned over the past few years: that the once
valueless franchise had a very high value now, in excess of two
million dollars—but only somewhere else, for we had neither an
adequate facility for the new operational rules nor an economic
base for building one. That the logic seemed akin to *Catch-22* or
something from the Vietnam War, like destroying a village in order to save it, made it even harder to accept. When it came time
to extrapolate on its own reporting and editorialize, the Waterloo
Courier got caught in this same spirit of conflict. In a statement
by assistant sports editor Doug Newhoff, the newspaper took a
bizarre position: Because the Waterloo Diamonds belonged to the
people of Waterloo, they could not be sold, but because they were
privately owned, public funds could not be used to help keep
them here. Strange logic, and almost completely contradictory,

but conforming with the screwball way the whole affair had developed.

In the end, faced with the prospect of having the ball club moved away immediately because the city was holding off renewing our stadium lease, I tried one last purist idea: Save baseball for Waterloo, at least certainly for 1994 if not longer, by giving our franchise back to the Midwest League and letting them come to terms with the city. With personal profit no longer a distraction, solutions might well be found. My motion was rejected— overwhelmed, with the only vote in favor being my own. Politely and with full assurance that I did not wish my philosophical difference to affect my respect for them or my friendship, I asked my fellow board members to accept my resignation. They did. A few days later, as reported in the press and confirmed in Richard Panek's book, the city demanded an annual rent payment of half a million dollars. The league now stepped in to declare the operation had to be shifted to Springfield, Illinois, where suitable terms and facilities were available. But by that time I was quite thankfully out of the picture.

As I write, Waterloo doesn't have a minor league baseball team and probably never again will. One of the unaffiliated independent leagues that have become popular of late looked us over and said nothing doing; we just don't have a chance to draw enough attendance. But neither does Springfield have a team; after two unsuccessful seasons there, what used to be my club moved on to immense success in a state-of-the-art new stadium built to bring them to Lansing, Michigan, where antidotes to rust-belt decay seem to have been found.

What was written about baseball in Waterloo began with optimism and ended with anything but. In *Basepaths* and *Waterloo Diamonds*, only the good are punished, and only the most innocent suffer. In the pages of the Waterloo *Courier* these days, not just sports operations but any development ideas are compared with the ball club's embarrassing debacle, a ball club that not so long ago could have both the newspaper's sports editor and editor in chief serving as board members with no conceivable conflict of interest. In a variation of what Richard Panek noted, all the owners had to show for their intentions were bitter memories and an empty ballpark. Would "fond memories" as the payoff for "noble intentions" (p. 133) have been any better? Only if baseball idealists were willing to pay their own way, something all three narratives find unlikely.

Box 28

FOR my first couple of years at the park, I didn't sit in the boxes. That night late in the 1977 season when I took the kids out to discover minor league baseball, we gravitated toward the place I sat when I was their age, when first getting closely involved with the sport.

One third up the grandstand, halfway between home and first: That's the place I picked when I had the picking. Not at Milwaukee County Stadium, where the Braves madness of the 1950s left choices only between the distant right field section and the towering upper deck. My chance to get a better seat and have it every time came ninety-one miles south, on Chicago's South Side, where at slimly attended weekday afternoon games in Comiskey Park I could get a kid's price general admission seat that in Milwaukee would have been in season ticket country.

Plus the atmosphere was a lot less heated at Comiskey, the going much easier for everyone on these series-ending getaway days when the visiting team, the umpiring crew, and perhaps the White Sox themselves would be looking forward to a travel date and wanting things less hassled. My grandmother would take me down on her railroad pass, set me off southward, and herself board the northbound Clark Street trolley that took her to a cousin's apartment up on Irving Park Road. That was just a few blocks beyond the Cubs at Wrigley Field, which I'd pass in the late afternoon when returning to meet her. Being out of town made baseball my whole day, and having it be the American League variety in an old, darkly shadowed park cast the experience as even more exotic. I must have done it thirty or forty times between ages nine and twelve. And now, with an eight-year-old son and six-year-old daughter, I was about to begin doing something much like it again.

Waterloo was another city, just seven miles from our home in Cedar Falls but a world apart in economics and demographics. As opposed to the college-town suburbia in which we lived, this was rust-belt industrial, a gritty town that even in Iowa managed a significant black population and plenty of other urbanisms. The park, too, was old and gritty, with enough crumbling mortar and peeling paint to remind me of Comiskey at its funkiest. Plus my own situation was in a state of change, just recently divorced and with custody of the kids. All in all, it seemed a good time to reach out for something different.

I'd been estranged from baseball for a dozen years—even a bit longer than that in thinking I'd outgrown it but most bitterly since 1965, when the Braves had turned traitor and left Milwaukee, carpetbagging their way to Atlanta. Now, estranged myself, I'd come back to a much earlier relationship. To my great surprise and pleasure, I was welcomed by what developed into a large extended family. Some were ballpark regulars, a few were members of the civic group that ran the operation (whose numbers I was soon invited to join), while a couple were even newer to the experience than I was and came at my behest. What drew us together, what made our point of unity, was not just a baseball game but the context in which it is played.

The game itself has this family appeal, if you give it the tending it deserves. Folks who see just one or two ball games a year are like orphans, their ballpark experience having the special nature of a day out, a holiday trip to realms not often visited. But go there for most if not all of the schedule and the team becomes

Box 28 101

familiar and personalized as a family, from the paternal manager, avuncular coaches, and solid, established players to the younger-sibling rookies showing inexperience at every turn. There are comfortable roles that make acquaintanceship easy: the rangy third baseman, the little spark plug at short, the loping outfielders, and the stocky, powerful catcher behind the plate. It's all a fabrication, of course—an especially artful combination put together by a general manager or farm director, all of it meant to have baseball played attractively and well. As such, it makes voyeurs of the fans, who because they've seen Ryne Sandberg perform so aptly in his role of star-second-baseman-who-can-hit, think they know him as a person. It's fake, it's phony, and it works. Neither fans nor players would have it any other way.

Come to sixty or seventy ball games a summer—even forty will do—and a truer, more genuine relationship builds among the people with whom you sit. Granted, this could be as artificial as bonding with Ryne Sandberg, for we were sitting not around a kitchen table but in a municipal stadium. Those first two summers, looking down on the main walkway that skirted the boxes and took people to their grandstand seats, I couldn't help but be struck by an attractive young woman there most nights: splendidly combed hair reaching to her waist, long bare legs climaxing in the shortest denim shorts conceivable, and absolutely basking in the glow of attention that followed her all the way to her privileged box seat. I didn't know her from Eve, so my familiarity was purely voyeuristic, as fabricated as could be.

Along the way she'd pass a rather grotesque-looking hunchback who was there every night as well. He too was interesting and became familiar. It seemed appropriate that these extreme examples from the stands knew each other, or at least said hello every night. As did a third figure, an old black man well into his eighties, whose enthusiasm styled from a much earlier era made him stand out among the cheering crowd.

I didn't know him personally but felt very comfortable, even secure, in his presence. He had a role, inoffensively baiting visiting players as they trooped in and out of their dugout just below him ("I'm gonna put my *thing* on you, you better watch *out!*") and chanting "Balk! Balk! Balk!" every time a pitcher tried holding our runner close.

When he died, his absence was noted—most obviously during high points when he would have led the cheering but more affectively in small, subtle ways.

"You know, I really miss Jon Shannon, you can tell he's not here," one of my friends in the boxes noted later, halfway through the first season without this old man at the games.

"Right," I agreed. "Their pitchers have it a lot easier now, and our rallies seem less intense."

"No, I mean right now," he corrected me.

I objected that the park was quiet, everyone subdued as a rather boring pitcher's duel was stretching into the late innings with very little action at all.

"That's what I mean," my friend said. "Just listen. What are we missing, what would we be hearing right now, with everyone so silent?"

"You're right!" I realized, remembering the muttered rhythms that would come drifting down from the old guy's position just over first base. "Aye, y'aye, y'aye, y'aye, y'aye," he'd murmur, sighing for all of us in our collective languor. It was missing right now—something missing not from the game but from the ballpark we all shared. Someone in the family had died, and his absence was a starkly sad reality with a presence all its own.

Maybe missing old Jon Shannon was a spectator sport as well, but the emotion was generated by things that happened on our side of the line. If not a family matter, it was neighborhood business. And the way my friend Larry noted it, it came from a sense of shared reality, a feeling that there had been a significant change in our common world. As for Jon's seatmates, his loss was surely felt as a very personal matter.

My first couple years were spent among one of several loosely knit groups. In open grandstand seating, the season ticket holders were bunched in little gatherings distributed here and there. On

Box 28 103

big nights when the park was full, they got lost in the crowd, but most of the time they were quite evident: Bill Boesen, his wife, and friends just opposite me between home and third; stately, white-haired Lefty Dunsmoor and his old friend Mildred Boyenga across the aisle from me and three rows back; Jack and Barb Kuper with their lively cheering section, the Zoo Crew, out in the bleachers just beyond first base; and five or six other knots of regulars spread around the park, always in the same place.

I knew the names because at the center of each group was a baseball board member pictured in the program. But I didn't need a program to identify the man and his family sitting right behind me. George DeMuth was a retired John Deere worker who'd been on the board for several years, almost as long as he'd been bringing his whole gang with him, including his wife, two daughters, a son-in-law, and several grandkids. By the end of that first short season in 1977 he'd not only become a friend but lined me up for season tickets, a legitimate money saver given how many games the kids and I took in. Halfway through 1978 he invited me to join the board and sponsored my membership. It was only when he died and his family stopped coming out that I satisfied a longtime urge by upgrading my tickets to first row box seats.

I picked them out a week before 1981's Opening Day, testing out various locations and viewing angles with Marshall Adesman, our new general manager, whose New York City background and Woody Allen manners had here in Corn-Belt Iowa broadcast his need of a friend. Among a baseball board of factory workers, fry cooks, and other tradespeople I looked like a safe harbor for his worries. What was a college professor doing on this board, he'd ask, and I told him they wanted to take a chance adding someone with a high school diploma. Acting like he expected a pogrom at any moment, he followed me around and only got into more trouble. Just the week before, as the more capable board members and their builder friends finished off the new concessions stand, Bill Boesen had sent Marshall and me off to buy a vent pipe for the cooking grill. After scouring every hardware store in the county, we returned three hours later with four types, all of them wrong. That made us "the stove-pipe crew," a joke I kept going when asked to MC the season ticket banquet. Among the gag awards I handed out was an exhaust joint to Bill, who right on cue grumped that it was still the wrong kind. Setting me up in a comfortable box was something Marshall was able to do, and after patient examination of everything available, he made me feel good about taking three seats right across the low cement wall from the visitors' on-deck circle.

With so many empty seats to choose from, I should have known it was going to be lonely down there. Box 28 had four chairs in the first row and another four in back. Across the little aisle within our steel railings were the eight chairs of Box 27, set up just the same. Sixteen seats were thus corralled together, but besides ours only two of them were taken. One, right next to me, was occupied on Opening Day by an older woman who introduced herself as a recent widow, coming out to the game alone for the first time. Sadly, she gave up less than halfway into the season. Behind her on the aisle was an even older man, who'd had his name tag cemented on the chairback. Mr. Stokes, as I called him that whole first year, was pleasant enough, and he came to every game but most often stayed absorbed in the play-by-play. He too had a sense of loss about him, though the nine innings of baseball seemed adequate recompense, at least for the two or three hours they filled.

In retrospect I have to wonder what Lee Stokes thought of me that first season in Box 28, for as subsequent years put us on a first name basis (and eventually much closer than that), I came to regret some of the more boisterous behavior I brought to what had been his quiet, contemplative part of the park.

For one thing, I was feeding the kids there, and for the first several innings our boxmate had his view obstructed by much coming and going for hotdogs and brats, pizza slices and nachos, popcorn, pop, and after all that a trip or two for ice cream. All the while I would have been putting away tall cups of easy flow-

Box 28   105

ing draft beer, often in the company of friends I'd brought out to the park for a night of loud hilarity. Sometimes these guys and I would smoke cigars, and innings would pass without attending to the game. It must have been no fun to sit right behind all this. Today, were such shenanigans to start in front of me, I'd scowl and change my seat. To his great credit, Lee Stokes never frowned, moved, or said a thing. When I did notice him, he'd just be sitting there cocked back at a comfortable angle, studying the pitcher's selection, noting how the batter shifted weight, and almost surely wondering when I'd start growing up and appreciate all there was to see.

Though in time this Mr. Stokes became a central family member in Box 28, it didn't happen that first year or even the next, though the pleasure of seeing each other next Opening Day after a long winter made for some shared fortune. Well into his seventies, pretty widely experienced and well traveled to boot, he had seen enough friendly associations come and go that he was not about to break out the balloons and party favors after just one year or two. Besides, he had his own little extended family joining him from time to time in our largely empty box. And what a family they were, drawing still others down here like flies to sugar.

Rather than a family, in fact, it was more like a harem. Because he doted on their interests, bought them bingo cards and popcorn and an occasional beer or Pepsi, players' wives and girlfriends found Lee Stokes great company. Not that they'd want to take advantage of him: Each time he'd pass out the bingo cards and solicit orders for snacks, they'd say he shouldn't be spending his money like this, that he'd really been too generous already. Then he in turn would dish out the commodity they really did love him for: his understanding. Not so much just sympathy for their plight of running a household on their husbands' measly pay—$630 a month at this level of the minors—or appreciating how their own educations and careers had been put on hold for the duration of this baseball lark or understanding the pressures of being moved around a farm system with no financial allowance for lost security deposits and hookup fees for phone and utilities or of being away from home for the first time in their lives. It was that Lee Stokes comprehended their situation, could give them good advice about handling their troubles, and seemed so downright fatherly here in such an otherwise alien world.

For his part, Lee certainly didn't mind being surrounded by up to half a dozen beautiful, sharply dressed young women. Their husbands or boyfriends had been the best athletes back home; they in turn were the great beauties. To anyone in the stadium, it was obvious that they adored Lee, and that was what he liked— not so much the adoration itself as the acclaim it brought him among the regulars, most of whom would have given far more than the dollar for three bingo cards and fifty cents for a drink to become the center of such attention.

Hence there would always be an old-timer or two who stopped by the box to tease Lee about his bevy of chorus girls, just to be able to sit among them for the half inning that custom allowed. With the kids not using their tickets on school nights I'd have the seats free to bring out friends of my own, and for them the baseball wives were quite an attraction. Jim Knowlton, a young modern languages professor with girlfriends across Europe, feasted on what he considered their inane chatter. Hal Wohl, a much older history professor but also a confirmed bachelor, didn't mind the chatter a bit—these were frankly gorgeous women, and to his mind they could say whatever they pleased. A few others were drawn by the chance to hear inside gossip about the team. And what gossip it was, all the way from the farm system's organizational politics to why the center fielder's wife put him in the doghouse after this last road trip.

When our GM, Marshall Adesman, came down for an inning, we had a real brain trust here, stretching from the occasional airhead baseball wife through a director whose expertise lay in keeping the beer bar's profits up to a somewhat frazzled general manager who acted like he'd taken the wrong subway line and come out in a hostile neighborhood full of Wonderbread eat-

Box 28 107

ers. You only had to sit with us for a few minutes to realize there was only one person in the vicinity who really knew what was going on: Lee Stokes, who'd been sitting in this seat almost since the park was built.

It was because we began respecting his wisdom that Lee finally blessed this little family's existence and took on the role of patriarch. A retired grocer, he told Marshall how years ago he'd helped run ballpark promotions with Eagle Food Stores, an account that since Eagle's departure from the area had been lost. Why not get Hy-Vee, their one-time rival, out here now for the same thing? (The key was winning numbers taped under certain seats—Lee remembered spending an entire afternoon with the butcher and the produce manager down on their hands and knees, sticking them on.) He had lots of baseball stories for me and my friends, luring us away from beer and cigars with better reasons to be out here. And to my kids he began acting like a grandfather, curious about the little events transpiring in their lives that parents too often take for granted.

Second to join us was Hal Wohl. More than anyone he loved the old-timeyness of the park's atmosphere, much of it reminiscent of the Ebbets Field of his childhood. The fact that another Brooklynite dropped by each game made it even better, and he and Marshall had much to compare. True, a generation in age separated them. Plus they'd attended different high schools: Marshall at Erasmus Hall near home, Hal traveling over to Manhattan each day for the academic magnet of Stuyvesant. But Brooklyn lore is timeless, and that Hal had spent the past thirty years out here in Iowa only made him more fascinating to Marshall—how had this fellow survived in such a strange, strange land?

In fact, Hal Wohl was so thoroughly New York that even to a practiced eye he could look like he'd only arrived yesterday. Teaching at the University of Northern Iowa since getting his doctorate in 1954, he'd never bought a home; in this community with precious few apartments, he'd rented for three decades, probably paying for his place on Campus Street twice over. Until recently, he'd never owned a car—because, until last year, he hadn't bothered to get a driver's license. We teased him about this endlessly, even when there was a serious matter invoked, such as when the house two doors down from me on Clay Street came on the market.

Didn't Hal want to buy it? The idea stunned him, even as I joked he'd be the first person in his family to own property in over three thousand years. I assured him the house wasn't on land claimed by the Palestinians. Still, no dice. Finally I promised to do some work on it, raising it up a story and putting a deli underneath. I'd even construct a subway line from Clay Street down to school.

This last point gave him pause.

"Express or local?" he asked, as if I had been serious. To Hal, the distinction was a key one.

Those first years, Hal came out a couple dozen times on the kids' tickets. Around school he had the reputation of being pretty tight with a dollar; bachelor that he was, living cheaply came naturally, together with having full control over each penny that went out. Hence he surprised me when during one spring's season ticket drive he offered to buy his own seat.

And so he did. But to everyone's further surprise, he insisted on saving twenty bucks by taking one nine rows back in the grandstand. Didn't he like our company, I chided, or was he really a loner at heart?

"Twenty dollars is a big difference for the same baseball game," he insisted, and bought in for sixty rather than eighty bucks.

So for two summers running we went through the same silly routine. Half an hour before game time, there would be Hal, taking his solitary seat up behind us to our right. One of us would go fetch him, explaining each time like reinventing the wheel that one of the kids or someone else wasn't coming tonight and he might as well use their seat, it was paid for. He'd join us, but stuck to the pattern for a couple of years until he began dating Jean

Box 28 109

Lund, the woman he'd eventually marry, and for respectability's sake bought first row seats next to me in Box 27. Coincidentally, I'm sure, this was the year Hal turned sixty and qualified for the half-price senior citizen discount.

By now Marshall Adesman had moved on, as our entry-level general managers were expected to do, becoming business manager for *Baseball America* magazine in Durham, North Carolina, where publisher and club owner Miles Wolff was helping create minor league baseball's suddenly booming popularity. Our new GM, Jim Peterson, was just as loyal to our box and doing an even better job of finding a half inning or so to sit with each little clan of hardcore fans, making everyone feel inside the operation. (Do they teach these things in school? Maybe so—Jim had an MA in sports administration from Western Illinois University, whereas Marshall's schooling had been to qualify for his previous job, writing program notes for WNET, public television in Manhattan.)

So the group remained intact and began developing lore and legends of its own. Baseball wives regenerated their collective presence each spring; Lee would get letters from some of the old ones now up with their husbands in Double A. Hal picked up the habit of bringing out junior colleagues; becoming an Assistant Professor of History at UNI now meant seeing games at Waterloo Municipal Stadium and hearing how much it was like the good old days at Ebbets Field. Harry Zanville, the only Jewish attorney in town, bought season tickets behind Hal. He did it for civic reasons and saw only a few games each year. But he became a perfect audience for my jokes on Hal, including the famous Willie Wilson story we also played out for Hal's new guests.

We'd lay the groundwork for it by steering talk around to the ballpark's last glory days, earlier in the 1970s when Waterloo had Kansas City's farm team that eventually grew up to be the 1980 American League champions. Hal McRae, Amos Otis, Clint Hurdle, Willie Wilson—everyone but the faster tracked George Brett, they'd all played here. As Wilson's name was mentioned, Hal would wince, knowing what was coming next.

"You guys saw Willie Wilson play?" the newcomer might ask in wonder, and Lee would chime in with stories about the kid's spectacular play.

"Of course it wasn't always like that," I'd butt in, and continue with a cock-and-bull fabrication about how Willie Wilson owed all his success to Hal.

"Those first few weeks of his rookie season," I'd say, "had the poor fellow really down on his game."

"You mean he wasn't hitting yet?" our involuntary straight man would ask.

"Oh," I'd croon in sympathy, "it was a sad, sad sight indeed. Willie could hit, all right. He'd line one off the left field wall but then be thrown out in a relay play at first. . . . "

"Willie *Wilson*?!!" the fan would interrupt, not believing what I'd said but eager to know this minor league lore nevertheless.

"You bet," I confirmed. "It would be worse when he walked. Next guy up would hit a clean triple, but Willie would be thrown out at second base. Oh, it was just terrible."

By now the Box 28 visitor was dumbfounded, especially as everyone else was playing along, grooming him for the coup de grace.

"One night before the game, Willie came over to the screen"—I indicated the backstop just before us—"and opened up his heart to Hal."

"Really?" the fan asked, wondering if from this would come the explanation.

"Oh yes," I confirmed. "Willie dragged himself over here so morbidly that Hal had to ask him what was wrong."

"He did?"

"Oh yes," I replied and, with Hal's manner and deeper inflection, began stroking my beard and speaking in tones of great probity, a mimicry praised by all as the best Hal Wohl possible.

" 'Why Willie,' Hal said, 'whatever can be wrong?' "

" 'Oh Mr. Wohl,' Willie replied, 'I'm so disappointed in my play that I think I'll just quit baseball and go home.' "

" 'Don't do that, Willie,' Hal countered."

Box 28 111

" 'But Mr. Wohl, you've seen how poorly I'm doing.' Indeed, Willie looked so dejected that Hal could have been his last friend on earth.' "

Hal, meanwhile, would have pulled his cap down and been staring forward with that same steady look he'd assumed up in the cheap seats each night before we'd invite him down. Which was my cue for the punch line.

" 'Now Willie,' Hal told the beleaguered kid, 'why don't you try something different?' "

" 'Something *different*, Mr. Wohl?' "

" 'Yes, Willie—try running faster.' "

" 'Running *faster*, Mr. Wohl?' "

" 'Yes, Willie,' Hal told him, 'run as *fast* as you *can!*' "

"And the rest?" Hal prompted us, looking up, smiling at the part of the story he liked best.

"And the rest," I repeated, "is history."

Amidst everyone's groans, I'd go on with a similar tale about a dejected young Mick Jagger telling Hal how his band called The Rolling Stones was boring audiences to sleep and how Hal told him to "*Jump around* when you sing, Mick, *jump around!*"

By now, Box 28 had established itself as one of the ballpark's islands. On quiet nights we'd be an oasis, miles of empty seats separating us from the nearest group of regulars. During big promotions, when the place was awash with wandering strangers and wild little kids, we were a safe harbor—this being season ticket country, free coupons didn't apply, and friends seeking us out knew there'd always be a couple of open chairs among us when every other seat in the park was taken. Hence we'd see a bit of Don Kruse from the Waterloo *Courier*, Dan McCool from the Des Moines *Register*, board members who wanted a bit of club politics, one of Hal's former junior colleagues from the History Department or a friend of mine from English, and of course Lee's covey of heartbreakingly beautiful baseball wives. Plus of course my kids, who were getting a great human education at the same time they were seeing more professional baseball games than any other youngsters ever.

That the sense of extended family was real got proven when the core of our group decided to do some things away from the Waterloo ballpark. Our cohesion was portable, we found, as long as it involved baseball. The same good times could be packed in a car, driven three hundred miles for a long day out, and dragged home together at something like three in the morning, all of us as comfortable as we'd been in our seats in the minor leagues.

Like the Box 28 experience itself, these travels started with the kids. With cable television had come Chicago Cubs baseball, and with the Cubs was Harry Caray, broadcasting in a style quite entertaining all its own but now coupled with an appealing, inviting ballpark and a sometimes exciting team. It had been thirty years since I'd been at Wrigley Field, but the place still looked the same. Seeing it again on TV, I wanted to be there and to take the kids along.

The drill was simple. Get up early, be rolling by daybreak. That would get us to Wrigley by ten-thirty, where I could buy pretty good seats for this afternoon's game—corporate season ticket hysteria would not sell the place out until the club really started winning at the end of the eighties. Then we'd drive to the North Loop, park for the day, and get an early lunch at Gino's. Next an "El" ride back to the ballpark and a full afternoon of baseball. After that, back to North Michigan and the car. Full of deep dish pizza from lunch and mounds of ballpark food, something light from the Vie de France bakery café at Water Tower Place would hold us for the long drive back to Cedar Falls.

Next stage was trying out Comiskey Park. By now the Chicago trips had been done in various combinations, one time or another including Hal, Lee, the kids, Don Kruse, or a UNI colleague/ballpark friend. It was a special thrill taking Lee along, for his experience made a perfect bookend to that of the kids: Whereas they were seeing these Chi-town locales for the first time, he was revisiting them for the first time in fifty years.

Lee's first trip in with us was to Wrigley Field—not his side of town, he cautioned us, but something he'd enjoy nevertheless.

Box 28 113

The gang was a small one: just Hal, Lee, and me, with Hal driving. It was one of those three o'clock starts, popular for getting a quasi-after-work crowd out to the park in the days before Wrigley had lights. So we had plenty of time to get there. But Lee and I had not reckoned with the habits of someone who'd only begun driving in his late fifties. Here we were, heading out of town on Highway 20, four-lane divided and limited access right up to Interstate rules and standards, and Hal was setting his speed at forty-eight miles per hour.

We tried kidding, but he was dead serious. In his book, a posted speed limit was like the red line on his car's tachometer: an absolute, stratospheric top limit, like as high as a NASA rocket could climb or as deep as an oceanic diver could plunge without rupturing eardrums and bursting lungs.

At this rate we'd wind up crowded out in the middle of Gino's noon-hour rush, not to mention being bored stiff by this turtle's crawl across the vast prairies to Chicago. All the coaxing in the world could only get him up to fifty; as soon as we'd stop urging him, he'd ease back to forty-eight, where his Volkswagen Rabbit had worn a groove. Then Lee started talking about the old days and things sped up. I mean *really* sped up. Only later, after it blew up in our faces, as it were, did I realize that Lee had talked this way to get Hal's foot down more firmly toward the floor.

Lee's tales were not, as I thought they'd be, just about Chicago, though that's where they started. As a young man back in the early 1930s, he'd had a job cutting meat for food service at the University of Chicago. Those were the roots of his South Side days. We asked him if this job had taken him into the world of college life, but it happened that his involvements were more shady.

"I'll never forget coming home from work in the late afternoon, waiting for the elevated train at 59th and Englewood," he reminisced. "Boys, you could stand right there and watch a parade of the world's most beautiful women walking right by!"

"Why was that?" Hal asked, keeping an eye on his speed.

"Because it was the shift change, boys," Lee answered with a trace of amusement.

"Shift change?" I queried. "Was there a factory nearby?"

"You bet there was a factory!" Lee cackled. "Biggest darn cathouse in town, right around the corner on 58th. They ran that place around the clock, 'cause at the stockyards or the railroads there was always somebody coming off. Well, about 4:15 in the afternoon, the girls were, too: first shift leaving, second crew coming on!"

His blood running faster with interest, Hal began letting his emotions drive the car. By the time Lee got into the next set of details, we were well into the redline territory of fifty-five mph, with sixty a real possibility.

Did he ever go there? Well, he'd had a look once or twice.

"Ground floor was like a great big dance hall," Lee explained. "All along one end of it was a bar, best stocked bar you ever saw, and of course anything you wanted was free."

"No kidding!" we both enthused.

"And all along the other side, boys, here were the women—most beautiful women in the world, as I said, and every one of them was naked, so you could see what you were getting."

Hal wanted to speak, but it seemed his mouth had gone dry. So he compensated with a few more miles per hour.

"And what you'd do," Lee continued, "is pick out the gal you wanted, take her over for a drink so's you'd get to know each other, then walk her on upstairs."

"Which was where . . . " Hal tried to say, but couldn't. I looked over and saw we were approaching sixty-five.

"You'd pay a fellow at the stairway two dollars," Lee advised, ignoring Hal and savoring his memory's own momentum. "One would go back to the girl, the other was for the house." He paused a bit while Hal tried moving his lips. "Pretty good system, if you ask me."

Hal finally did find some words after Lee digressed into stories about a less interesting vice, gambling. How he'd been able

Box 28 115

to open up a card room by paying off the cops—"There'd always be one fellow, called 'the Captain's boy,' who'd come see you for the money," Lee recalled. I was intrigued when he got to the story's point: that bribing the police was just half of it; you had territorial rights to worry about as well, especially as this was neighborhood turf of the Capones.

"Mimi Capone, Al's little brother, came to see me one day," Lee smiled. "After a very enlightening discussion, he made me see the wisdom in moving very far from Chicago!"

"And that's how you got to Cedar Falls?" I asked.

"Well," Lee chuckled, "Mimi said don't stop driving 'til I ran out of gas, and as you know, that's about as far as a tank will take you."

"So that was the end of your experience with the world's most beautiful women?" Hal asked, obviously disappointed.

"Boys," Lee laughed outright, "there are beautiful women everywhere! Some of the best I've seen were out in Reno, Nevada. Ran a little bar out there for a while, had to move on after the tax agents and I had a little disagreement about the labels on my whiskey bottles. . . . Lost some money on that, lost even more on some bad debts owed to me. But the girls out there . . . "

"The girls?" Hal prompted him to remember.

"Working girls, you know," Lee winked. "They had the biggest hearts and the most honest characters of anyone I ever met. Would lend them money lots of times, you know, and not a single one of 'em ever failed to pay me back."

Sitting in the back seat, leaning forward into the conversation, I saw something glinting in the rear view mirror. Something flashing, something red. Looking down to Hal's speedometer, I saw it indicating seventy-five. These images of the honest working girls of Reno, Nevada, would be Hal's last innocently happy thought of the day.

In fact, the ticket turned out to be not that bad at all. The state trooper was impressed that this was a sixty-year-old gentleman's first-ever stop for speeding; Lee and I kept quiet about how new his license was. Though Hal was twenty miles per hour over

the limit, perilously close to reckless driving, the trooper knocked
the violation down to sixty-five—that would mean a thirty dollar
ticket instead of sixty. As we resumed the trip (at fifty-five), Lee
and I pulled out our wallets and gave Hal ten bucks apiece, our
fair share. Gassing up in Illinois, we teased him in front of the
station attendant, calling him "old Hotwheels here," and learned
the sobering fact that *any* moving violation this side of the river
cost a hundred dollars minimum. So it was a good thing Lee had
talked about the cathouse on 58th Street and the hookers with
hearts of gold and matching credit ratings while we were still safe
in Iowa.

Lee loved Wrigley, got a kick out of Gino's, remembered his
own long-ago rides on the"El"—all in all a good, happy trip, even
though his seventy-eight years made the wee hours of our return
tiring (six hundred miles with a ball game in between!). For me,
the best part was coming in on the Kennedy past O'Hare when
the skyline first looms into view.

Here was this old, old man, whose last view hereabouts may
have been looking back over his shoulder to see if the Capone
brothers were on his tail, surveying such sights as the Sears
Tower and John Hancock building while the freeway let us bar-
rel through a slice of old neighborhoods in his day negotiated at
pushcart speed.

"What do you think?" we asked him. His reply was slow and
measured.

"I can see they've made a lot of changes," Lee said and then
was quiet for several minutes, lost in thought.

It was a summer later that Lee Stokes reclaimed the Chicago
of his young manhood, proving to himself and to us that despite
all the freeways and skyscrapers, not that much had changed.
This was for a night game at old Comiskey. My ex-wife, now
working for a law firm in Chicago, had access to eight box seats
right over the Sox on-deck circle, so we didn't have to buy tickets.
They even came with a coupon for preferred parking, so we didn't
need to take the South Side "El," though I'm sure Lee would have
loved it.

Box 28 117

The group this time was Lee, myself, my son Jonathan (age sixteen at the time), and one of Lee's baseball wives, Jackie Githens. Jackie was, in Lee's book, a gift from heaven: lively, entertaining, gregarious, and quite an activist when it came to taking advantage of circumstances. From the season's start, she took absolute delight in Lee's amenities and within a week was bringing things like home-baked rhubarb pie for Box 28 to enjoy. When we planned our Chicago trip, she joined in without hesitation and enthused over every small detail of it. Gino's she loved, borrowing a felt pen to write her husband's name among the millions that filled every flat surface in the place.

"John Githens, number twenty-six," she announced with a flourish. "When he's pitching for Cleveland and they're in town, we'll come here and I'll show him this!"

Yet for all Jackie's excitement, the trip was really Lee's. A ballpark kid and baseball wife were his perfect audience, and having been refamiliarized with Chicago he had the confidence to play his patriarch's role. In busy Gino's, where we had an early dinner, he was able to get Pepsi refills for Jonathan and Jackie in a flash; in a crowded, understaffed dining room, his was the glance that could catch a waiter's every time. On Michigan Avenue, heading south at rush hour, he flabbergasted me with his manners on the street, rolling down his passenger-side window to bark at the cop untangling the gridlock at Congress, "What the hell's the matter with you? Where'd you learn to direct traffic?" As I cringed, the officer just looked down at Lee, smiled, and had the best laugh of his day.

At Comiskey, which Lee hadn't seen in over fifty years, he marched us right up to the gates and with a practiced eye asked me what we were going to do with the extra four tickets. Brushing away my worries about being nabbed for scalping, he took the unused four and taught Jackie how to peddle them, letting her keep the forty dollars earned (though she insisted on spending half of it on our ballpark food). Entering the park, a ticket taker asked us if we were all one family. I was about to say yes when Lee cut in and said we were three—he'd already noticed it was a giveaway night, smoke detectors of all things, one to each family. Without a question, the guy gave us three. I hope Jonathan and Jackie were taking notes.

That night in old Comiskey Park was so much like our evenings back home in Box 28 that I wished the experience could last forever. As happens so easily at ballparks, we made friends with the folks around and, by the night's end, felt we'd all known one another for life. Yet rather than miss the big league excitement of Chicago, it made us more appreciative of the even better life we had in the park at Waterloo. More family members, more diverse and yet even more integrated into our group. More stimuli, more adventures, a wider arena for action within a much smaller stadium, simply because we knew it so long and so well.

In time, the group grew even larger, until every seat of the sixteen there was filled. The fourth chair in my own front row was purchased by my barber, Larry Peters—it was Larry who'd so tellingly note the absence of the old black gentleman, Jon Shannon, a few years later. Behind me, next to Lee, sat a junior colleague I brought out, following Hal's example: Jeff Copeland, who in coming years would be tenured, promoted twice, and finally became department head, beating out Hal's protégés by light years. An elderly couple who vaguely knew Lee filled in the back row, while next door in Box 27 the just-retired personnel director for John Deere, Ray DeBarr, bought tickets for himself and his wife and began spending afternoons doing volunteer fix-up work around the park. A lawyer, who became my own, Steve Weidner, took the seats next to Harry Zanville, and down in front Hal astonished everyone when he bought out the whole first row so that he and his new wife could bring friends every night. This made it a quite radically extended family, but we all got along famously. At a ballpark, how could you not?

Each year, as the short season of minor league baseball ended just before Labor Day, we'd hang on for a while afterwards, letting the stands empty out before making our own farewells. Hal and Jeff I'd be seeing at school, Larry every three or four

Box 28 119

weeks for a haircut. But Lee—Lee Stokes was someone we knew only from the ballpark or trips to other games.

"See you next spring!" we'd tell him and always get the same reply.

"The Good Lord willing, yes," he'd tell us, and I knew the prayer and the reality behind it were sincere.

That Lee would be there every Opening Day didn't alter the fact that one day he wouldn't. That day came a few years later, when for the extra chilly home opener his seat went unoccupied. As a month went by with no evidence of our patriarch, we made inquiries. Larry's friend Bill Dillon knew Lee from other associations: Bill's father-in-law had been Lee's partner in the grocery store business. According to Bill, Lee had suffered a bad winter, was bouncing back, but because of eye surgery couldn't trust his vision to drive, especially at night.

Heck, Hal or I could drive him. Why didn't he let us know when he was ready?

A week later, with the warm weather that finally arrived toward the end of May, Lee appeared. Talk about a grand entry: We all but stood and applauded. As it was, we surrounded him with handshakes and backslaps and chidings about where had he been. We hardly noticed that he'd brought a young kid with him—or rather that the kid, a neighborhood teenager, had been hired to bring Lee.

Pleasant as the kid was, it was clear that baseball and our Box 28 habits bored him, so his summer job lasted just one night. For the next day's game I made arrangements to pick Lee up, brushing off his worries that it was going out of my way, and for the rest of this year and the next, either Hal or I made sure to promise him a ride for each subsequent game.

What had ailed him? "Boys," he told us, "I had everything, everything but the clap!" There'd been kidney problems, some heart congestion, and a lung infection that he thought was sure to kill him. He'd been in and out of the hospital half a dozen times and still didn't feel much better. But he'd gone ahead with the eye surgery and enjoyed telling us how the laser machine his doctor used cost ten thousand dollars for every quarter of a second.

With Lee back, Box 28 became happily overcrowded. My friend Mildred Boyenga, who'd been club president for several years and actually won a Baseball Woman of the Year award at the Winter Meetings, changed seats and took over one of the kids' chairs—Nina was not yet back from her junior high school year at a lycée in Paris, and Jonathan was staying in Iowa City for summer college classes and a job reporting sports at the newspaper. As I'd kept up their season tickets anyway, to maintain our hold on the box, a young university librarian named Tim Wiles took advantage of the free seat and made himself a regular—fun for us, because his previous job had been as an intern at the Hall of Fame's National Baseball Library in Cooperstown.

By summer's end, with both kids back for a while and everyone enjoying the good weather, we had a fully represented family down here, with individuals of every age from baseball wives' babies through teenagers and people in their twenties, thirties, and forties to Hal and Mildred in their sixties and Lee pushing eighty. Because it was structured as a family, everyone knew his or her role and was comfortable in it. With Lee having flirted with disabling bad health and survived it, we hoped our style of baseball could go on forever. Or almost forever.

Our tacit assumption was that Lee would go first. That was our downfall—and his, too. The reckoning came a week or so before opening day in 1992. Our preseason ticket drive was winding down. New seats had been sold; old ones were being renewed and delivered. In the club's little shotgun chamber of an office, behind the ticket window and next to concessions, our general manager called me aside. He was just starting his second year on the job but already knew all the knots of regulars by heart—and was justifiably alarmed when a patriarch of any of these clans turned up missing.

Our new GM's name was Dave Simpson, and his twangy Kentucky voice made his message sound even more jarringly out of place.

Box 28 121

"Jerry," he summoned me. "Y'all heard about Mr. Lee Stokes from your box?"

"No," I answered, fearing the worst. "Is he . . . ?"

"Waall," Dave drawled, "we've learned his seat is going to be available this year. Ah thought y'all'd want to know that."

"Oh no," I moaned, "is he too sick to come out at all? He didn't die on us, did he?"

"Mr. Stokes's health is just fine. But there has been a death. We understand it was his wife."

"No way, Dave," I argued, actually relieved a bit at this obvious confusion of events. If Lee was okay, his wife certainly was, for she was twenty-five years younger than him.

I knew this because Lee would boast about her; plus I'd met her at the door when calling before the game. She was in her early fifties and looked great, even to having stunningly long red hair. From the start, Lee had always reveled in the great life she gave him, telling us of roasts simmering in the oven to feast him after Sunday afternoon games, mashed potatoes, real gravy, strawberry shortcake for dessert. . . . No, Lil could not be dead. Dave surely had the story wrong . . . Maybe it was Lee who died, I reasoned—and suddenly realized that if one of the two had to go, better it be Lee, as he'd always assumed would happen, for the thought of this colorful but weakened old man living without her was unbearable.

By Opening Day, we still hadn't confirmed the story. In other circumstances Hal or I would have gone by his house or, at the very least, called. But our extended family's life was based on baseball. We came to existence at the ballpark or, at the very most, during a trip to one of Chicago's ballparks, and never before had any of us violated that code by seeking someone out in real life, as it were. Real life was what we left behind, with our own real families, when we came out to the game. Comingle the two, we feared, and each would lose its appeal. Certainly ballpark life would lose its magic.

If what Dave said was true, Lee Stokes surely didn't want us to see him in either life right now, terrible as things must be.

There were discreet ways of inquiring, and we took those routes. My barber, Larry, had his friend Bill Dillon ask his father-in-law. Jeff Nelson, our personable new assistant GM, claimed he'd met someone who knew Lee from the business world and promised to look into the matter. Before long, we had the truth, and as feared, it wasn't very pretty.

Lil Stokes, aged fifty-two, had died of a heart attack, totally unexpected. Lee had taken it very hard—indeed, it had just about destroyed him. For a while, his life had been a shambles. Then a sister living on the West Coast had invited him for a visit, and that's where he was now. Word was to expect him back in town by June.

It was actually late in May, around Memorial Day, when I spotted the old four-wheel-drive truck Lee used for snowplowing—even at eighty, he was always working little deals to make a buck. Here he was driving down 18th Street in Cedar Falls, cursing at traffic and looking his old self.

At the stoplight a tardy driver had made him miss, I pulled up next to him, leaned across the seat, and called to him through the open window.

"Hey, you're back!" I cheered, deciding this was not the time or place for condolences but rather for looking to the future. "We've kept your seat warm—when we gonna see you?"

Lee smiled, which raised my spirits immensely.

"I'm not quite ready yet," he called back, then paused as if in thought. "But you boys'll see me! Keep her warm!"

And that was it.

Weeks went by without him. Jeff Nelson heard he was planning to move to his sister's out West, that he was getting his house ready to sell. Then the other old-timer in our box said he'd heard Lee was sick again, delaying his move. It began to seem less and less likely that we'd see him at the park. But his seat was saved nevertheless.

Finally the bad news came from Bill Dillon, out with his friend Larry for a game, largely to give us the word. Lee had been out one night, later than he should, and had tripped on the side-

Box 28 123

walk to his house. His head struck the back steps, sharp concrete cracking his skull. He'd lain there unseen all night, blood soaking into his brain. A couple weeks in the hospital saved his life, but he was now in a nursing home, never to leave.

"We can't bring him to games?" I asked.

Bill Dillon shook his head.

"Well, what home is he in? We really should go see him!"

Again, Bill shook his head no.

"Why not?" Hal and I asked together.

"The home doesn't want visitors," Bill explained. "Lee's too far gone to recognize people or remember them, and when he tries to, it gets him real upset."

"Oh no . . . " I murmured.

"He wouldn't know you," Bill said, then added more quietly, "And you wouldn't recognize him."

Family life continued in Box 28, but for everything that happened, I couldn't help regretting what Lee missed. Most of the good stuff involved the kids. During high school, Jonathan had brought the senior jazz group out one year for Opening Day festivities, and Lee got a kick out of seeing a fourteen-piece dance band, the orchestration of his era, spread out along three rows of the grandstand, Jonathan playing lead tenor sax. Even before this, Lee had encouraged the kid's other avocation, writing sports features on the ballclub for the local shopper paper (and earning five bucks a crack for his efforts). Now he was a young man living in Iowa City, coming back to a few games each summer to give updates on his true careers now: writing sports and editing for the Gannett newspaper, the Iowa City *Press-Citizen*, and as a self-taught guitarist leading his own successful, well-paid blues band, good enough to be booked as far away as St. Louis and at Buddy Guy's Legends club in Chicago.

As for Nina, who'd delighted Lee with her business acumen and aggressive drive, recycling beer cans and hawking popcorn in the stands, her success was even more typically in this old operator's style. The first years of it Lee had followed with pleasure, cackling with glee as her story unfolded: dropping out of college first semester, bussing to Chicago to try out as a telemarketer and testing so well that she was hired on the spot as a shift supervisor. From here, already doing well enough to rent a nice apartment on Lake Shore Drive ("She's on the Gold Coast!" Lee had cheered), she'd attended court reporting school and became certified. It was the first year without Lee in our box that she returned for a special visit, bringing for introductions her fiancé, a young but already established Chicago attorney. After seating Ralph among us, there was only one place left, and Nina hesitated to take it. We told her Lee would want her there, owning his old Chicago as she did. She took his place respectfully, but with comfortable presence.

The other things Lee missed were not so pleasant. But I still wished he'd been there, as perhaps he could have prevented or at least ameliorated the trouble. The whole mess involved the ball club, and what a mess it was. For the decade that I'd been involved, the operation had suffered its ups and downs, a couple of times facing serious problems. In 1988 we'd lost our affiliation with Cleveland and had to scramble for a co-op team to tide us over for a year until San Diego could be persuaded to take us on as their mid-ranked A farm club. Another hassle involved getting properly incorporated, something that in our offhand way of running this not-for-profit organization had been neglected and then forgotten. But in 1991 Major League Baseball had put some rigorous new rules into effect, shifting more operating expenses to their minor league partners and setting up strict new standards for playing fields, facilities, and stands—none of which we could meet without massive cash from the city, something totally out of the question.

Lee, to his credit, saw it coming well before any of us. Way back in the mid-eighties, before Cleveland's pullout and the incorporation mess, he sat there in Box 28 one night with a wary eye cocked toward Dan Yates, a new board member who'd shaken up the old ways of doing things and gotten himself named chair of any number of new reorganizational committees.

"Looks to me like Mr. Dan Yates is bucking to be president

Box 28 125

of Waterloo Baseball," Lee noted, watching the guy popping from seat to seat, glad-handing everyone.

"Oh, he's just a new enthusiast," I argued, dismissing Dan's behavior as just his personality.

"Don't be too sure about that," Lee warned, reminding me that when I was a new board member ten years before I'd kept pretty quiet 'til I'd learned the ropes and the ropes learned me.

He had a point. And from the way his brow was furrowed and his glance narrowed, I knew Lee was drawing on a lifetime of such observations, all the way from getting caught between the police and Al Capone's mob in Depression-era Chicago to tangling with revenue agents in Reno and running grocery stores out in California and here in Iowa. He had a great talent for showing disapproval, and he was surely indicating it now.

Within a year, Dan Yates was president, surprising everyone but Lee. And shortly after that things started getting bad with the club. It wasn't Dan's fault by any means. It wasn't anyone's fault, just a case of the city going broke just as the major leagues got greedy. Coinciding with both was Dan Yates and his new leadership style, which took a hard-nosed attitude toward business (which we needed to survive) and an equally strident position with the city (which didn't help at all). Meetings with the city council and park board about stadium improvements became confrontational. So did our monthly business sessions. Board members squabbled with Dan, with the GM, and with each other.

Lee saw the start of this during his last year at the park. I could tell he didn't like it as I sat there in the first row of Box 28 alternately politicking and anguishing with colleagues who'd drop down to discuss the latest management crisis.

A wry sense of irony also settled in the box that last summer with Lee. He himself got quite a chuckle out of our paradoxical financial situation: that going broke, as it was, the club couldn't afford the new improvements being mandated and might have to be sold; but if it were sold, we'd all be rich, as even defunct franchises were changing hands these days for three million dollars. The old gent really had a good laugh when Hal stepped forward to save the day. Years before, he'd declined an invitation to join the board because of the ten-dollar membership fee. Now he was ready to fork over that double sawbuck for the privilege of becoming an owner and only blushed slightly when asked if he'd figured out what was one-fifteenth of three mil.

Overall there were relatively few such laughs. Instead, anxiety over the club's fate led to dissension, and dissension to recrimination. When it finally did come to an end, it was even worse than we'd imagined: a legacy of stress that left at least two heart attacks and any number of health problems among board members, lifelong friendships placed on hold if not completely sundered, and a hideous image for us among the fans and townspeople we'd meant to altruistically represent.

Even the climax was an unforeseen disaster. The best scenario would have been for the club to be sold to new ownership who'd fix up the park and keep baseball here. Goodness knows, there were plenty of monied interests around. But no dice; nobody wanted the club, a multimillion-dollar asset, even for free. One local group said they'd take it over if we paid them a hundred thousand dollars to do so, as an indemnity against possible debts. No wonder Waterloo was sinking; how many great deals were being lost because of such venal selfishness? Worst of all, we on the board were being perceived as just as bad, if not worse.

So what happened was the worst of all possibilities: The club was sold and moved; plus the sale money was held in escrow by the league when the city, claiming it owned the franchise, threatened to sue.

At least Lee wasn't there to see it or for me to endure his glaring scowl. For all in the world he had seen, I'm sure there had been worse—but also that in his wisdom and experience he'd done much better with it. That was the big difference on our board of directors: So many of the old-timers had passed away. Gibby Gibson, who ran a sports trophy store and any other number of small businesses, died two years before. Lefty Dunsmoor, in his seventies and still on the board, was battling prostate can-

Box 28   127

cer and had less time for the club and its problems. Others had moved away, with no one really to replace them.

These were folks who'd been with the club since the 1940s and 50s. In that time they'd seen plenty of ups and downs and had developed the smarts to weather them all. Our own generation just didn't seem to have it.

These days there is still baseball of sorts in Waterloo—an amateur summer college league has a team here—but no more Box 28. Maybe it all would have ended anyway: Lee Stokes lost to us, Mildred Boyenga moved to Florida, Bill Dillon off to a string of cabins he and his friends bought along the good-fishing Wapsipinicon River, my kids living their own adult lives in Iowa City and Chicago, and so forth. But not even the box remains. In their first year the new Northwoods League club renumbered all the seating and subsequently rebuilt the lower boxes with new-style chairs left over from the hockey arena going up across town. Narrower and shorter, they made it possible to fit two more seats in each row. Any extended family in Boxes 27 and 28 would now have to number twenty instead of sixteen. Twenty sounds less like a family than a mob.

The new team gave us former board members season tickets, most of which I give away. But two or three times each summer I take in a game. A couple UNI friends have taken up support of the team, and I usually sit with them. If other old colleagues from the minor league operation use their season passes, they're coming other nights than I do.

Here and there I recognize a few knots of regulars from the old days and even a few groups who've become Waterloo Bucks fans, as the team is called. But I'm not one of them, not knowing the players by name or reputation, not following their fortunes well enough to know if what's happening that night is significant or not.

Number 17 hits a hard grounder down the line for a stand-up double. Is that better than usual or par for the course? I don't know. Even with my seatmate of the night, there's nothing to discuss, because the particulars are Greek to me. I'm just an orphan here.

Most nights I wind up leaving early, walking past what used to be Box 28 on my way out. It's really spooky how nobody sits there, some of the best seats in the house. I haven't yet and surely won't, for if I did, I fear I'd disappear.

Mildred

IRST time I saw her was at a baseball meeting, sometime toward the end of the 1978 season. She was the only woman up there at the front table and stood out for that. But she also had attractive looks, especially for her age, which seemed to be mid-fifties.

Arched eyebrows, perky hair, sharp features, and a very alert manner with an air of half skepticism, half intrigue. She bore more than a little resemblance to Lauren Bacall and also to the 1940s stripper Pepper Powell. What a combination, what a range of fantasies, all of them definitely period—the period when I was a little child. The minor league baseball club held its board meetings in the back room of a tavern, and as she sat there at the officers' table, cigarette in hand and drink at her elbow, she seemed posed for a scene with Bogie or in sufficiently alluring shape to get up behind the bar and dance.

She was club secretary and had been for some time, a natural enough position for a woman to assume back then. There were others among the forty-odd board members, and in time a couple of them would assume equal prominence. But for now Mildred was the only standout in this world of hustling small businessmen and beefy John Deere line workers who ran the club.

I'd been invited to join this board after attending less than a season's games. That's how loose the organization was, how informally it treated the idea of someone becoming a part owner. Not that the club or its franchise was worth anything. Since the end of the 1950s, minor league baseball had been in decline, and the Waterloo Indians, Cleveland's affiliate in the Class A (second from the bottom) Midwest League, was a break-even operation simply because its local ownership took no money out of it and instead volunteered their own services rather than pay wages to others.

I'd drawn notice by being at the games every night and making regular appearances at the beer bar. That was the club president's work station, and he seconded my nomination with the endorsement that he'd noticed I was "a good beer drinker." Mildred looked up at this, laughed, and said she was putting that in the minutes. On this note of good humor, I left the room while membership voted and, on my reentry, was congratulated and invited to buy the drinkers at the front table a round.

It was good to be accepted, for there was nobody else like me on the board. They were all Waterloo people for one thing, involved in the city's blue collar/small business life, which seemed (and was) so distant from the wealthier college town qualities of Cedar Falls, where I lived and worked. That I was a university professor got conveniently ignored; looking at these old minutes today, I'm amused to see how Mildred had logged me in as "a teacher in Cedar Falls." Fred Hahn coached football at the Catholic school, Columbus High. Barb Kuper was attendance clerk at Hoover Intermediate, and Lana Morgan supervised the study hall at East. As I didn't work at Deere's or sell real estate, it was among them that I was being classed, which was just fine with me.

There were other board members I came to know before Mildred, and it wasn't until I brought my wife out for some games that she took notice, making friends with her before getting close to me. The folks who felt affinities with this "teacher in Cedar

Falls" who looked and dressed more like a part-time laborer were the board's odd crew of semi-degenerates.

Some of these people were real characters. A few years before, a hotel manager had got himself elected club president by packing the board with his employees: not just reservation clerks and office staff but maids and kitchen help, even the lowly dishwasher. This last poor soul had ailments head to toe, inside and out, including some obvious brain damage. Yet in the goodness of his heart, he was the first to make me feel really welcome, and so I returned the allegiance well past the time our board slimmed down, spiffed up, and began trying to ease him out. He in turn had his own clique of friends among our fan base, and they were colorful indeed, including Tex, lean and mean looking in cowboy hat, boots, and even spurs, who lived at the Salvation Army shelter, and Greg, who dressed like I did and looked as though he didn't have any home at all. These guys I'd help out with free tickets and an occasional couple bucks, always "just a loan." As Mildred got to know me, she'd be critical of how I "encouraged" them.

Mildred's own crowd was the business group. She herself was in middle management at Rath Packing. An old Rath salesman, Lefty Dunsmoor, was her closest friend on the board, but she seemed to know everyone who wore a white shirt and tie in Waterloo. She got along with the factory workers, too—with Deere booming and the union strong, they earned as much as any realtor or hotel manager and were accepted for their economic clout. I tended to fall in with the factory types, guys who reminded me of my background in Milwaukee, where the breweries (for which my father sold) and big plants like Heil, Perfex, Harnischfeger, and Square D dominated everything.

For most of those years in the late seventies and early eighties, the club ran on its own momentum. The larger board existed for two reasons: to elect the officers who constituted an executive board, which made all the practical decisions, and to sell season tickets and various coupon-book packages. We had something for everyone, from an entire corporate box (eight season tickets for something like six hundred dollars, for which the only customers were a couple of banks and John Deere headquarters) to little stapled items called the Individual Book and the Family Book: fifteen separate tickets for as little as twenty dollars.

Board members had their season ticket customers lined up year after year. Allegiances were respected, and no one trod on any one else's territory. It was so protective that this practice sometimes hurt the club; more than once an old board member died taking his list of steady customers with him, not even his widow or children able to crack the secret for us. When a few years later a new, business-oriented general manager proposed letting the office make a central directory, the outcry was phenomenal. People prized their sales records, the totals for which were published each week during our preseason ticket drive. Cash prizes—significant ones, as much as five hundred or a thousand dollars, went to the contest winners, usually those with the best corporate contacts. But even the rumdums could compete. If you couldn't sell an eighty-dollar season box seat or even a twenty-dollar Family Book, we had booster buttons: little tin pin-ons with a Waterloo Indians logo, date, and fresh annual slogan. These were peddled for a dollar. For some of our members the year's big event was the button kickoff, when you'd start from our meeting place at the AmVets Hall and do a pub crawl to virtually every other bar in town, accosting friends and strangers, pumping each for a buck purchase.

In return, button buyers would be admitted free on scheduled button nights: just a couple each year and usually on hopeless dates like a cold weeknight in April or the day after the Fourth of July, times when the park would be mostly empty otherwise. Goofy as it was, this practice was treasured, and you could always find a fan or two at the games festooned with every button issued for the last twenty years.

Mildred, needless to say, was not a button bash person, though she always wore hers during the ticket campaign (it was a dollar fine to be caught without one, collectible as you purchased a replacement from the fellow member who'd caught you). Her ticket sales were high enough to place her among the winners, her customers the type of regulars you liked to see—out there every night, patronizing concessions (if only for a cup of coffee, the senior citizen staple), getting to know the players and helping them out with loaned furniture and sometimes cheaply rented rooms. As with her disapproval of my palling around with the degenerates, her motive was always to make minor league baseball in Waterloo more serious and respectable. Which makes it ironic indeed that we became friends, as my own impulse was always toward the operation's funkier and more comic aspects.

Though she wasn't an instigator of reform, it was a couple of new members' disgust with club shenanigans that made Mildred Boyenga an agent of the process. It started when two unlikely people got involved and almost at once began agitating for change. One was Dan Yates, a very clean-cut, energetic, almost Eagle Scoutish community relations specialist for the State Sheriffs Association. Before this, he'd been involved in Christian radio; so you get the picture. The other was Ruta Zemaitas, a classical harpsichordist who with her graduate degree had taught music in college. Believe it or not, she had been hired a few years before as our assistant general manager, coming from wealthy Grosse Point Park, Michigan (where her father was a prominent physician) to realize her girlhood Tiger-fan dream of working in baseball. She had done a good job for the club and did well herself, marrying a fan and starting a family. When she left the assistant GM job, she asked if she could stay involved with the board, to which she was welcomed. At which point she teamed with the other new member, Dan Yates, to clean the operation up.

Not that there was any truly dirty business going on. Anyone looking to skim profits would have to find a much deeper till than Waterloo Baseball's. We handled a lot of money but spent a lot too, basically breaking even. But there was some mostly harmless funny business, the kind of stuff that happens in any organization where folks can too easily congratulate themselves for working for free.

For example: Any food left over at season's end was divided up among the members who helped out at concessions. This was reasonable enough, as no way could the perishables be kept seven months until the gates opened again. But the slick stuff involved placing an order for eighty pounds of bratwurst, for example, on the last game date of the year. Some items were ordered that we didn't even sell so that a few cronies could be eating free ribeye all winter. Compounding the offense was that the current club president managed our concessions stand—not for any salary, mind you, but rewarded for not wasting money by being given 10 percent of what was netted after costs.

Here and there a couple board members were earning a few bucks, mostly for assuming duties that had to be formalized beyond the happenstance of volunteers, such as ushering and serving as public address announcer. Pay was minimal, five or ten dollars a night. But it was pay nevertheless, an inequality that Dan and Ruta deemed unfair.

They came to a board meeting with objections. The club president was surprised and offended but made a classic mistake. Instead of letting the issue be introduced amid the board's confusion and die for lack of forethought, he thought to silence them by appointing a study committee, to consist of Ruta and Dan. Next meeting they returned all primed and loaded for bear. Their carefully drafted proposal fell on well prepared ground, and all but one board member voted to end the 10 percent bonus and prohibit any of us from being paid at the park. The single vote against it was mine—not because I'd earned money or got free food but because I didn't like sleeping dogs aroused in this cheesy way, smacking so much of petty organizational politics. In truth, I enjoyed the notion of these ham-fisted line workers cooking up their silly little schemes and hated to see this bit of local color being washed away.

As I feared, the board's decision tore things up. Jerry Heber, the club president, resigned. That made his John Deere coworker, Craig Twaites, president—at which point Craig resigned. That left the lowly club secretary, someone who'd had a place at the front table simply by virtue of shorthand and typing skills. Mildred Boyenga was now president of Waterloo Baseball.

I'll never forget how she moved to the table's center and took over the job—shaken, and at the edge of being distraught, but pulling herself together to maintain this organization about which she so deeply cared.

"I guess the first thing is we need a new secretary," she announced, getting a few laughs. "And a treasurer," she added as an afterthought. This wasn't going to be easy, she must have known. "The floor is open. Do I hear some nominations?"

There were none, everyone still shocked by the angry exits.

"Come on, people!" Mildred urged, sounding for the first time like someone in command. "We have to keep this ball club together; we can't let it all end like this."

Someone nominated Barb Kuper for secretary. Dan Yates put in Ruta's name for treasurer. That was it. They were elected by acclamation. Only later, when it made the national press, did we realize that we were the first entirely woman-run professional sports organization in America.

The old executive board's last act had been to hire a new general manager, Jim Peterson, and Jim's first act was to call our major league affiliate in Cleveland to report the change. Bob Quinn, as traditional a baseball man as there ever was, old style from the word go, reacted even more violently than we'd feared.

"Mildred Boyenga?!" he squawked, hearing who was now in charge. "That shriveled-up old chicken? What the hell's going on up there?" Instability among local ownership was the main reason farm teams changed cities back in those days. Attendance wasn't their concern, and stadium conditions were uniformly shabby around the minors—the boom in bush league baseball was still many years away, and most ballparks dated from the last time minor league ball had been popular, which was the 1920s and '30s.

Bob Quinn had yelled at us a few years back about our bus, a rattletrap affair that he honestly feared was endangering the players—or rather putting at risk Cleveland's big investment in their top draft picks. His crowning argument was the many hundreds of thousands his club had paid outfielder Dave Clark. We could lease a brand new bus for every season 'til the end of the century, Quinn lectured us, and not come close to paying what he'd paid for one draft pick in one year.

He got his new bus lease and Cleveland stayed in Waterloo. But we could see why he was worried now about Mildred. Bob Quinn's farm system budget was under six million dollars, with a million and a half of it committed to Waterloo. And it was local ownership who was responsible for spending upwards of a million of that budget and spending it right. We had to lease the bus, book motels, distribute meal money, and have airline tickets ready when players were moved during the season and sent home at the end. We even had to buy enough baseballs, in orders of twenty dozen at a time, to make sure games could be played. Plus there was our own expense and expertise for maintaining the field and keeping the stands sufficiently safe that the fire marshal didn't close us down. All Bob Quinn had to do was pay the players, which at $630 a month apiece for just five months was the cheapest line in his budget. The really important stuff, stuff where things could easily go wrong and often did, was in our hands—in the hands of this "shriveled-up old chicken" that he, like all the other men around, had known only as a competent secretary.

Fortunately, with Opening Day just weeks away, all went well. At least so far as Bob Quinn could see. Obstructions thrown up were petty and local. Some of the old officers' season ticket and book customers didn't renew, and the AmVets Hall, where we had our monthly meetings, asked us to take our business elsewhere—not because they were friends with the old leadership but because they didn't want to be seen as taking sides (a boycott by the John Deere crowd would have broken them). So we moved a couple miles east to their rivals, the Veterans of Foreign Wars club, downtown next to the Golden Dolphin Show Lounge. For the rest of our baseball lives we lived with the reputation that comes from having one's car parked during happy hour right outside a strip joint.

By the time of his annual visit in mid-June, Quinn seemed comfortable enough with Mildred's leadership that he could attend to real business, which meant deciding which of his second- and third-year veterans should be released to make room for the new crop of players just drafted. At the time, we were Cleveland's only Class A club. Two-thirds of their new acquisitions could break in with the rookie league team in Elmyra, but the rest— mostly college players—had to come here.

A couple of our guys might be promoted to Double A in Chattanooga. That was the happier part of Bob's visit. But the sight of him sitting there in the lower box seats flanked by his director of player personnel and one of the more experienced roving instructors was intimidating. Heads were going to roll. Players played nervously, doing poorly under pressure—just the thing Quinn and his associates were there to note. Wives and girlfriends were even more on edge; you could tell whose mate was on the bubble, for chances were that night they'd stay away.

But in Bob Quinn's book, Mildred was accepted. Here in the third month of the season, there had been no bungled reimbursements or botched reservations. He'd had no player complaints and—more significantly—no bad words from his manager, coach, or trainer. In fact, talk was that Waterloo was being run quite well, far better than the rumors heard about the place last year. We all knew Quinn was pleased when he set off happily for the Hickory House for his postgame pow-wow, as he called it, with his cigar-smoking Waterloo cronies, our oldest, most traditional baseball types available—and invited Mildred to come along. Shriveled-up old chicken indeed!

She hit it off with Quinn easily enough. They were of the same generation—Bob the no-nonsense style of businessman she'd always admired, Mildred the type of tough little broad he knew from past experience was thoroughly reliable and your best fighter in a pinch. The fights, a couple of tough ones, would come a bit later, tangles threatening the very existence of the club that made our initial leadership hassle seem quite petty indeed. But first there was the issue of Mildred's empowerment, to use a

current word that surely gained its meaning through the efforts
of women Mildred's age.

Winning Bob Quinn's respect had a lot to do with it, though
Bob himself would never assume she had to struggle. When con-
veying his ultimatums to the board, she'd always do it with a great
sense of seriousness. We had to do this, we had to do that—she
made it damned clear to us that you didn't mess with this hard-
nosed pro. But when she faced him herself, you'd never guess that
Mildred wasn't every bit as tough as he was. Which was true.
Sitting around the VFW club with her ragtag baseball board, she
knew full well how weak we were and how any number of vulner-
abilities could make our operation collapse. We were, after all, a
literal house of cards, a construction of just three sheets of paper:
a stadium lease, a league franchise, and a player development
contract with Cleveland. At present, only the third was of any real
value, and Cleveland itself was one of the wobbliest organizations
in professional sports. Only because they had a hard-as-nails person at the helm did their farm system survive at all.

But the same worked for us as well. When Mildred was facing Quinn directly, she gave no quarter. No matter that the Waterloo franchise was weak. *She* was strong, and it was Mildred
Boyenga and not a shabby circus known as Waterloo Baseball that
was sitting across the table from Bob. I suspect she'd picked up
the talent at work. Though employed in middle management at
Rath, she was a union member and an active one at that: on
the negotiating team when the plant ran full bore, part of the
reorganization committee when the company became employee-
owned, and even acting on the national level as a delegate to the
1972 Democratic Convention, the one that rewrote all the rules
and nominated George McGovern. Talk about lost causes. But
for Rath workers and McGovern Mildred had fought hard, and
whether facing bankrupting owners or Richard Nixon's dirty
tricks squad, you don't stay in the fight by showing weakness.

Talking turkey one-on-one with Bob, fresh from breakfast at
the Ramada Inn coffee shop and swapping tales with his whiskey
and cigar crowd at the Hickory House, Mildred did more than

keep up. On several issues she won Quinn over on points he hadn't wanted to compromise: better players from the draft, quicker turnarounds on reimbursements. But most of all she won his respect, which made her own job with the club much easier to do.

The other great empowerment came from an unlikely source: the new field manager, Steve Swisher. Swish was still young, a bona fide major leaguer just finished with a career that took him from the Cubs to the White Sox, then the Cardinals, and finally Cleveland. He had baseball cards and milestones in the game's history: being part of the Don Kessinger trade that established baseball's Ten and Five rule (giving players the right to reject trades once they'd been in the majors ten years and with a single club for five), then making himself notorious, along with Pete Vuckovich and Kenny Reitz, as the core of the rowdiest Cardinals team since the Gas House Gang. He'd finished up as Cleveland's bull pen coach, a job he dramatized as needing finely honed psychological as well as technical skills. He was big league all the way and eager to get back to the show. Managing, a challenge that was even more psychological, would be his ticket.

For a complex of subtle reasons, he and Mildred hit it off. Such was not usually the case when it came to club presidents and field managers. Duties and interests are so different that the roles could be at times adversarial, and a few years before a blowup between the two factions had been surprisingly violent. Jerry Heber, one of our beefier Deere workers, had still been president then. Easygoing manager Gomer Hodge (a name and personality to suit it right from central casting) was lax in controling his players, and one of them—catcher John Malkin—was notorious for breaking the rule against coming to the concessions stand after the gates opened.

Night after night, there'd be John, hulking in his uniform and tearing up our soft asphalt with his cleats, ordering enough junk food to feed an army. This night Jerry Heber had had enough, and frog-walked Malkin back to the clubhouse and into the manager's office.

Picture Gomer, lazy and lanky and drawling, "Hi y'all, what's up?" Picture Jerry, short and bald and aggressive, coming on like a muscular Don Rickles. And also picture an unsuspecting visitor, Cleveland's director of player personnel, Dan Carnavele, as old time and as scrappy as they come.

Never having met Jerry Heber and totally unprepared for his abrasiveness, Carnavele thought our president was the clubhouse boy. And how could a lowly clubbie be getting so big for his boots as to come on this way with a player and the manager? So Carnavele settled the matter according to his finest personal style, grabbing Heber by the throat, hammering a fist to his face, and depositing him semiconscious on the clubhouse floor.

I heard the story only later, after that night's game, during which an absolute sweetheart of a Dan Carnavele had made the rounds, grandly schmoozing with every board member he could find. Nothing much came of the incident, other than to remind everyone that a distance should be maintained between on-field and off-field interests. And that's why it was so unusual, with stories of Heber and Carnavele's prizefight still making their way through the Cleveland organization, for the new rookie manager to become such close friends with President Mildred Boyenga.

Though knowing Swish so well made Mildred even more capable as a sports professional, it was not her toughness that in this instance came into play. Rather it was another set of qualities: her long experience, her solid wisdom, and most of all her practical ability to share her knowledge in an effective, helpful way. Steve Swisher had come to Waterloo quite alone, as a rookie manager out of the major leagues after enjoying its privileges for more than a dozen years. For the first time in a long time, everything wouldn't be done for him; he'd have to do it himself, and it was all new. Plus he was not a rowdy goof-off but the boss who had to keep players like he once was in order. Mildred, also new at sudden responsibility, was a kindred soul, just a few miles further down the road than he was. Her help could be invaluable.

Swish was alone in another way: His wife and kids were not along. His working day was spent riding herd on two dozen young men, and for after-hours company he had just two more guys for friends, his pitching coach and the trainer. They'd left families at home, too, and after postgame workouts at the Nautilus gym and dinners with drinks at the steakhouse their collective lives must have felt empty indeed.

The simple pleasure of being able to sit and talk with a woman was quite appealing. That Mildred was old enough to be his mother didn't put a damper on it. No, to Swish her age meant that she was a leader, already something of a veteran at it, one who'd seen things through and could offer advice. The motherhood angle was a matter of tough experience: Among Mildred's children was a son badly wounded in Vietnam, with all the attendant problems of readjustment. Lord knows what she'd gone through in counseling him. Helping this reformed hippie learn how to whip a minor league ball club into shape would be nothing in comparison.

There had never been a Mr. Boyenga around, and in time I'd learned that Mildred was divorced. Her houseful of kids she'd raised on her own. Juggled with the responsibilities of her job and union work, motherhood must have been a handful, and it had made her an eminently self-reliant person. I know she prided herself on this strength, because she was not hesitant to credit the achievement. One time a friend of a friend was visiting our box and complained how although his marriage had deteriorated and divorce seemed inevitable, he just couldn't leave his wife with the job of raising their kids. "Why not?" Mildred challenged him, angry at his patronizing attitude. "*I* did it!" So on top of everything else, Swish had this to draw on from Mildred as well.

Family life was one of his and Mildred's topics. They'd be together at the far ends of a baseball day, sitting up in the shady grandstand in the mid-afternoon an hour before the players arrived, and bending elbows at the vendors' beer tap in concessions, finishing off a few by themselves in a darkened ballpark long emptied of fans and personnel.

Years later, after Swish's team had won the Midwest League championship and he himself had been promoted to managing

Cleveland's Triple-A farm club, Mildred would recall those long conversations. What had they talked about? Everything. How could he instill some seriousness in these eighteen- and twenty-two-year-olds whose idea of what they were doing amounted to high school sports without the books? How could he make them understand how precious was their opportunity?—how the value of these years was not in being able to live irresponsibly but to have a chance at doing what only seven hundred or so of three hundred million Americans could do at any time: play major league baseball.

Then there was his own situation: out of the majors, responsible for himself and twenty-five others, and not having a wife and kids to come home to after each road trip. Lil had stayed in West Virginia, where she was operating a clothes boutique. His little boys were in grade school, and couldn't be moved 'til June. Not that Lil wanted to move out to Waterloo at all. Her business was beginning to thrive, and her interest in it consumed attention previously given him. This mystified Swish, and Mildred was called on to explain it.

But more so than the players and even his wife, Steve Swisher had someone else he was struggling to understand: himself. Here was where Mildred was most helpful, not for what she did say but for what she didn't say. "I did a lot of listening," she recalled. But Swish wasn't talking to a fence post. Like a good analyst, Mildred knew that having an intelligent, experienced, and above all very wise person hear him out would help Swish learn what he had to about himself. He could speak freely and bravely, venturing into areas he'd never contemplated before. He didn't have to worry about making bad mistakes; Mildred was there to correct him if he erred, catch him if he fell. Sometimes he came close.

Knowing him only because he'd ask me regularly for stats, even I was able to see the mass of contradictions that he was. Everyone knew the stories about his misbehavior on that 1978–1980 Cardinals team with Vuckovich and Reitz. Despite their talents, the three had been traded to different clubs in 1981 in order to break up the ringleading that made their team the most unmanageable in baseball. Their pranks had been big time—it was probably the puny immaturity of his minor leaguers' attitudes that bothered this veteran of stunts still talked about years later. Most importantly, he and Pete and Kenny had never let it hurt their game. Their best production, in fact, was during a rainout, when the three had invited fans down on the field to slide around on the tarp and do belly flops in the mud. It had taken the full force of stadium security to break up, Swish recalled, smiling. What made him scowl was his own players getting drunk every night, showing up late and hungover and, even when sober, not paying attention to instruction or crucial game situations or just not trying very hard at all.

His Topps baseball card from that era showed an icon of the age: scraggly beard, long, bushy hair, and a wise-guy expression that implied the card shoot was just one more bit of foolishness to him. He looked like someone who needed to be taken in hand. Maybe his wife Lil had been the one to do that. But Lil wasn't here now, so he was turning to Mildred instead.

She couldn't have approved the contrary icon he'd installed beneath the glass top of his manager's desk, a full-color oversized picture of General William Westmoreland, who back in Steve's hippie days had been the American commander in Vietnam. His clean, stern visage may have been whispering now to Steve Swisher as a rookie leader, but to Mildred it could only bring to mind her adversarial McGovern politics and her son so deeply damaged by this General's war. Yet she never challenged Swish about it. What an odd source of inspirations he'd assembled, from eagle-eyed Westy to her. If the General could make room for Mildred, Mildred could accommodate him. It takes strange bedfellows to produce a successful rookie manager.

Especially considering where Swish was sleeping. When the team arrived each April, flying up from spring training in Arizona, Cleveland footed the bill for two nights at the Ramada or Twin Torch Inn. After that, they were on their own. This meant manager, pitching coach, and trainer, as well as the two dozen or so players. Apartments were hunted down from lists the GM had, leads supplied by fans who'd made acquaintances at the welcoming banquet first night in, or references gleaned from last year's Waterloo vets in camp.

For some reason Swish opted out of the great apartment hunt, choosing instead to bunk it in the tiny manager's office. Big enough for only his desk, a locker, and an old broken-down couch, it was just what he guessed he needed. The ticket seller had a little nine-inch television up front that Swish could bring back after games to watch *The Tonight Show* or *Letterman*. The GM gave him a gate key so he wouldn't be locked in. Meant to be a temporary arrangement, it persisted through April and May and into June. When his wife elected not to spend the summer out here, Swish might well have stayed in that rathole office forever, even without air conditioning or good ventilation.

What put Steve Swisher into an apartment was his kids. When school ended, Lil brought them out for a visit and, at her husband's and their urging, let the two little boys stay with him in Waterloo for a baseball summer.

Mildred delighted in Lil, recognizing a fellow self-reliant woman. But she also feared what the separation was doing to their marriage. As for leaving the boys, six and eight, to be raised in the working atmosphere of a minor league ballpark, Mildred suspected with some reason that the kids might wind up feral before the season ended and they got back with their mom.

It turned out to be not so bad. In town, Swish rented a two-bedroom place, and on road trips they tripled up in motels. Nights were late, frightfully late for their ages, but days were heaven. The kids were given batboy uniforms and would go out there tossing balls back and forth with the players, every one of whom wanted to be special for the manager's sons. The six-year-old, small for his age, was the more energetic of the two and by far the scrappier. One Sunday afternoon, when archrival Cedar Rapids had their own little batboy along, a fight broke out; and as fifty players crowded the field for pushes and shoves, Swish's little kid came shooting out of our dugout and tackled his equally tiny opposite number on the Reds' club.

Their summer was a boy's paradise in a man's domain, a realm almost totally devoid of women. Except for one, this much older person their father seemed to be relying on even more than his wife. Indeed, if Steve had ever been as candid with Lil as he was with Mildred, things would have been better for family life and other important matters these young parents had to determine.

It was about this time, still near the start of her presidency, that Mildred took on her weightiest task. She'd stabilized local leadership, kept tight with Cleveland, and seen her rookie manager project pan out well as Swish won the championship here, managed brilliantly in Triple-A, and got back to his beloved majors as a coach with the New York Mets. She'd proven herself pretty good at baseball, in both its political and personal dimensions. This new challenge, however, involved matters of business and the law. Fortunately, she'd worked with big-time lawyers during the reorganization and dissolution of Rath Packing, because our own situation with the club was turning out to be almost as serious.

Waterloo Baseball didn't make any money, but it handled a lot, almost a million going through our hands for sales and purchases and even more than that spent on the team on Cleveland's behalf. Seventy thousand fans would watch games in our park, sitting there amidst a summer of rocketing foul balls and safety railings that weren't very safe at all. We sold hundreds of thousands of beers to people in festive moods, hot dogs to kids who trusted they weren't being food poisoned, and cigarettes and cigars to young people we assumed were of age. A couple thousand cars played dodgem in our dusty parking lot. And so on. Here we were, Mildred found out, with our incorporation lapsed for twenty years and us handling all this dynamite with no protection at all.

We were even setting off fireworks on the Fourth in this

overcrowded firetrap of a park. At least we bought insurance for that. But our daily operations were a risk both financially and for liability. If anything went wrong, businesswise or with an accident, we individual board members would have to pay.

Plus in larger business terms the situation was even worse. When our incorporation lapsed so long ago, so did proper ownership of our Midwest League franchise. That had been allowed to happen because during minor league baseball's slide from popularity such franchises had become worth little or nothing. If no one cared, why bother? But during the 1980s the minors had climbed back, thanks not just to renewed interest in the majors but also to the very nature of that success. Major league baseball was popular but also expensive, distant, and overwhelming. The minors were cheap and intimate. Entrepreneurs got interested, franchises started changing hands for real money, and the escalation began. A worthless franchise sold for ten thousand dollars, then forty thousand dollars, followed by steady increments in six figures. By the time our own lack of papers became an issue, the first A-level club had sold for a million. Before it ended, prices reached three times that.

Not that there was any more money to be made locally. We were in a small market with a depressed economy, playing with a lackluster affiliation in a shabby, worn-out park. But there were others in more fast-track places who would love to have our slot in the league. Wisconsin Rapids had been pillaged for its franchise. So had Wausau. Others were in danger. Weak as we were, Waterloo was a candidate for this list. And now it turned out we didn't even have proper legal title to our club.

This mess had come about because as a board of directors we hadn't been very businesslike, much less professional. Because the club was small time and its challenges minor, momentum seemed the rule of the day. Things would carry on, and all we directors had to be was steady at the helm.

"Steady at the helm?" Mildred had exclaimed when some board members argued against her urgency. "I'd say we've been asleep at the wheel!" Lack of incorporation was a serious matter. Without it, we were operating at risk, even if the league let us continue.

"But we have a franchise," came the objection. "We've been paying dues."

"Yes, we've paid dues," Mildred allowed, "but we never paid for the franchise. And the corporation to which the franchise was issued back in 1957 no longer exists."

Years ago, such papers changed hands as a mere formality, often for a dollar plus good will. But with speculative interests having pushed up prices to over a million, the Midwest League had become a more than eager seller. Expansion franchises were created and sold for hundreds of thousands. In short order the lineup of clubs had grown from eight to fourteen. Given the number of major league affiliations available, that was about as far as it could go. If someone wanted in, they'd have to buy somebody out, at the recently inflated prices. Or, as Mildred soberly told us, they could have the Midwest League resell a franchise that by breaking the rules had reverted back.

"And the rules," she reminded us, "have been broken."

It should not have surprised us that in facing this crisis Mildred had already acted to get it resolved. She won the respect of Bob Quinn and became the major resource for Steve Swisher, and she hadn't done that by lacking initiative. But what she'd done now raised some concern, especially my own.

For all of its existence, Waterloo Baseball had been run by simple rules. The elected officers constituted an executive board; they kept a firm hand on operations, debated what should be done, and brought their recommendations to the full board on a monthly basis for ratification. Approval was customary, but not before any beered-up member could spend as much time as he wished blowing off his big bazoo about the wisdom or lack of it in the proposal, which could be as mundane as buying another fifty feet of garden hose for the groundskeeper. Such colloquies were part of our democratic image and are the chief reason why people get involved with civic groups and service organizations in the first place: to arise from their bland anonymity and spend a moment or many moments blowing off their big bazoos.

What Mildred had done prompted me to blow off mine. The focus of it all was her decision to go out and hire a lawyer for the club. In thirty years of operation, we'd never had one. Only recently had we even deigned to hire an accountant. We were unprofessional, and, even worse than that, we were cheap. Why pay for so-called experts when any of us could add and subtract and things were running pretty much okay anyway? But with this incorporation matter they weren't, and so Mildred, knowing the board would never endorse doing something that hadn't been done before, quite naturally acted on her own.

Spending seventy-five bucks to ask some questions of a local barrister would have been controversial enough. But Mildred had gone for broke by retaining a nationally known professional in baseball law, John Wendell of Lakeland, Florida. It was the Midwest League who recommended him, Wendell having consulted for them in the past. They were being generous, wanting to keep us in and willing to help us out. But only if we got things straightened out and restored to proper form, which wasn't going to be cheap.

At the meeting where Mildred announced her action I hit the ceiling, partly at the anticipated expense but mostly out of anger at her sidestepping of the board. We supposed insiders were suddenly on the outside, just when the most important piece of club business ever was coming to hand.

"Well," Mildred answered me, undaunted by my ire, "if you don't like it, tell John about it. He'll be here Monday night."

And so I did. Out of deference to his profession and status in it, we moved Monday's meeting from our usual tavern to a conference room at the Ramada. Mildred and her officers sat as usual at the front table, while board members filled several ranks of chairs. I was in the first row.

John Wendell might be costing us a million dollars, but at least he looked it. Tall, lean, fit, and just slightly tanned, with his striking gray hair but otherwise active looks he struck me as a senior tennis pro. A well-dressed senior tennis pro, for his suit alone must have cost more than all the other clothing in the room combined. Were he doing a commercial for Mr. Coffee machines, you'd buy one. Did he want your vote? He'd have it. And from the start he was prepared to win mine.

With hardly a word of introduction, I came at him like a pit bull. Was he aware, I asked, that he'd been brought here without board approval or even consultation? That we were skeptical of his worth to us and that without our approval he couldn't be paid, not even for his plane trip up here? Only my genuine anger kept me from showing embarrassment at how asinine I must have sounded.

To my bluster John Wendell replied with quiet courtesy and honest concern. Yes, we members had not been consulted. But from Florida he'd only had the chance to speak with our president. He was here tonight because he wanted to hear from all of us and so that we could hear him. How would it be if we suspended debate over payment until he told us what his proposition was and answered our questions about it. Then we could decide for ourselves.

Who could argue with that, especially as it had been proposed in a tone so caring and conciliatory as to make my own ranting seem worse than Hitler's. I settled down to see what would happen and found myself incorporated into his presentation as the ideal listener to his plans.

He'd asked for a blackboard and in a patient, professorial manner began diagramming the structure of franchise ownership and incorporation. His pedagogy was brilliant, his teacherly manner appealing. Within minutes he had the group fascinated, hanging on every word and stroke of his artful chalktalk.

The role reversal was excellent. John Wendell was no longer a flashy out-of-town lawyer, the shyster with a briefcase we'd feared would come carpetbagging in and clean us out. Instead, he was a fatherly law professor and we his law school students, eager to please him as we learned how to think like lawyers ourselves.

Before he was finished, all we wanted was to be someone like him: fit and trim, patient and gently instructive, quelling the rages of little Hitlers in the audience and letting us see how clear and simple the solution was. Every one of his points solicited and incorporated my point of view. Throughout the presentation he spoke to me not as an adversary but as if I were his best friend and most trusted confidant in the room. Attractive as he and his argument were, any person would be flattered to be considered so. I fell for it, as they say, like a ton of bricks, devouring his attentions hook, line, and sinker.

In pleasing fashion he explained just what forms of protection incorporation did and did not offer, a good enough lesson that I was able to use it with a local lawyer next year and be praised for my legal lucidity. Next came the hopes and hazards of establishing clear title to the club and its franchise. Finally, John Wendell told us all how to properly structure a corporation. The shocker was no more monthly board meetings with everyone blowing off his big bazoo. The board at present would become stockholders, gathering just once a year to elect a board of officers—about six was ideal—and let it run things unimpeded for the next twelve months.

There was more to John Wendell than this good presentation. In coming weeks and months he was back several times to direct Mildred's search of local and state records, establishing a history of Waterloo baseball. He helped pinpoint just when, where, why, and how the last incorporation had gone bad. That had been about twenty years before, when the board's nature had begun changing from a group of business promoters to the loosely organized gang of civic volunteers and social clubbers it was now. The incorporation documents as drawn up had been flawed. The State of Iowa had never accepted them. But so casual now was the club that no one ever noticed—or really cared to look, for that matter. After all, we ourselves had been operating year after year with never a thought for it.

As our high-powered lawyer led us through these thickets he kept his charm cranked up to optimum levels. A pilot, one of his hobbies was collecting and flying antique aircraft, and during a long car ride to a league meeting he regaled Mildred and some others with a hilarious story of trying to board a commercial airliner with his parachute, a chute he'd need when flying home the old open cockpit biplane he was going out to retrieve. When Mildred told him I was doing a book about World War II flyers in the Royal Air Force he began sending me bits of period lore, from a copy of John Gillespie McGhee's *High Flight* to newspaper clippings about lend-lease training bases in central Florida used by the British back then. If I came down, he offered, he'd take me out to some crash sites, even show me where I could pluck a souvenir from wrecked fighters and bombers. I never had the chance, but when the book appeared next year I sent John a copy and was rewarded with a thankful phone call. John Wendell was always making sure I remained his very special friend.

Through it all, Mildred worked on as leader. When John was in town, she'd let him do the talking, sitting aside with a deeply satisfied smile, pleased not just with his effectiveness but at how ably he was having me and other early skeptics buttered on his toast. When called back by affairs or to any of the other league headquarters that commanded his attentions and paid his fees, he let Mildred continue by herself, consulting at times with Steve Weidner, a lawyer who'd worked with her on the Rath settlement and the local representative John had helped choose.

As a piece of legal and business accomplishment, her success was unparalleled. Around the country and within our own league, clubs were being stolen away or going belly-up on their own for less serious problems. But thanks to Mildred and her choice of lawyers we came through it okay, our franchise rebestowed and clear ownership established. The operation was now called Waterloo Professional Baseball, Incorporated, and it was with pride and reverence that we spelled it out and always spoke the full title, never dropping our sign of legal status or just saying "ink."

We now had a six-member board, one of those elected being me. The stockholders may have thought I'd be a watchdog, but

Mildred knew I'd roll over like a puppy any time I'd have my tummy rubbed, like John Wendell had done. My job was to be club secretary, a role I interpreted as being resident historian. But everyone knew Mildred was calling the shots, and it was not long before national recognition for all she'd done followed.

An annual rite for both big league and minor league baseball is the Winter Meetings, occupying the first week of December in a warm weather location such as Dallas, San Diego, or most often Florida. For several days the exhibit halls are packed with displays of every possible piece of field equipment and advertising promotion. Entry-level candidates for management positions line up for interviews, while veterans work the lobbies for leads on coaching and scouting jobs. Here and there actual major league general managers rub elbows and swap players, but the overall atmosphere is social, anyone and everyone getting together to say hello and reestablish the fact that they're all in baseball. There are hospitality rooms, cocktail parties, and banquets large and small. One of the largest is the Recognition Dinner, where awards for this and that are handed out. One of the awards was for Baseball Woman of the Year, and Mildred Boyenga was the recipient.

"All I can say," she told the gathering that included everyone from George Steinbrenner and Peter O'Malley to Stan Musial and Henry Aaron, "is that I deserve this!" The line was pure Mildred and brought appreciative laughter and a sincere ovation. The commendation had credited her emergency assumption of the presidency and subsequent struggle to straighten out the incorporation. But surely she was thinking of all those late night talks with Steve Swisher, half a generation after similar counseling of her own war-shattered son, and of rowdy, sometimes unruly board meetings at the VFW Hall as she tried convincing a roomful of good old boy sports types that this reorganization business was serious, that she'd seen it all before at Rath's, and that the results might not be very pretty. At the Winter Meetings, her one-liner said it all. And everyone believed her.

Thus steered, Waterloo Professional Baseball, Incorporated, made its way through the balance of the 1980s. All went smoothly, with no overwhelming problems to solve; the next life-threatening crisis wouldn't come until the decade's end. But there was a very literal life-threatening crisis when an ulcer that Mildred had developed burst. We could easily have lost her; at the hospital's emergency room and then in its intensive care unit, Mildred's doctor warned her that the odds weren't in her favor, that her condition was acutely critical, and that she could be just hours from death.

Like everything else, she fought through it, even bringing others along with her. Our general manager at the time was smoking heavily, as had Mildred all her adult life, and had brushed aside some early warnings of stomach troubles just like Mildred's. Right there in the emergency room, in great pain and with her life in the balance, Mildred made him promise that he'd had his last cigarette.

"I don't ever want you to be here like this," she warned him, then added a characteristic touch. "I'm stopping smoking. If I can do it, so can you." They both did.

There were plenty of stresses that could have contributed to Mildred's medical crisis, anything and everything from Vietnam and the collapse of Rath to the challenge of saving our ball club. She'd fought for civil rights in Waterloo, home of a sizable African-American community, worked at Democratic conventions all the way to the national, raised a family on her own, and run the ball club through several of its tightest squeezes so far. Now, nearly written off for dead on the emergency room table, she'd dodged another bullet. This one, she decided, would be her last.

With everything well in order, she declined another term as president. Dan Yates, who'd joined the board just a few years back and at once began reforming everything, impressed her as a safe replacement. She'd been grooming Dan for the position, she assured us. Besides, she just couldn't stand any more hassles, however minor. She'd had enough.

It was lucky that she had, for within a year of her retirement, ball club matters went bad. This time it wasn't our fault. Because of its own reorganization, Cleveland pulled out; San Diego came in, first as part of a co-op, then with a full affiliation. This was not earthshaking, as working agreements were shifted around routinely in the minor leagues, the majors usually making sure somebody covered each stop. But more serious were the tougher standards being required in return. The stadium improvements mandated were way beyond our own abilities and the resources of our city. Struggling on was a lost cause, but struggle we did, through a deteriorating atmosphere of hostility and recrimination. It was good that Mildred was out of it, as there was nothing even she could have done, so hopeless was the situation.

Into these dire times for baseball in Waterloo came the last young man Mildred Boyenga would influence, at least in terms of working with the club. His name was Richard Panek, his occupation was being a professional writer, and his present task (for which he had a contract and publisher's advance) was to write a book about today's minor leagues. Waterloo would be his focus. He'd learned about us by reading my stories in *Short Season* and figured our operation provided the scope he needed. From New York, Richard didn't know about the specific economic developments that were putting our club at risk, but as it happened, these doings helped him fashion an uncommonly tragic plot. You can't have tragedy without a heroine, someone who gives meaning and soul to the inexorable action. For Richard Panek's book, Mildred became that figure.

How was he drawn to her? Like everyone else—Steve Swisher, Bob Quinn, whoever—Richard could see she had the smarts and the strength, the depth and above all the character. He'd been working for magazines several years, doing stories on truly important people and topics for everything from *Mirabella* to *The New York Times Magazine*. His training began at the prestigious Medill School of Journalism at Northwestern, but he'd developed more lyric talents at the University of Iowa's Writers Workshop. Northwestern taught him how to get the facts. The Workshop cultured his ability to find the soul and express it in language that wouldn't shame Flannery O'Connor or James Joyce. Mildred, as Swish and the others had learned already, had not only the facts but also the soul. There is no way Richard could have written such an insightful book without her at its center.

Though she's not mentioned at the time, her presence is evident in the volume's first lines, about how here in Iowa the eye inevitably rises from broad horizons to contemplate the vastness of the sky. Earth and sky, sky and earth—the rhythm that characterizes Richard's book is set on the first page. And the earth in question is not just farmland. Rather it's the land that people have worked and that now provides their eternal rest. An early scene takes place in a graveyard, the narrative counting off names on tombstones and associating them with business and community endeavors from Waterloo's earlier, better days. Though not mentioned, it was Mildred who took Richard to this cemetery, pointed out the names, and told him the stories that anchor his tale.

Waterloo Diamonds is the title of Richard's book as published by St. Martin's Press (New York) in 1995. But throughout his many long visits through the 1992 season and afterward, he did much more than spend time with the team. True, those twenty-five players wore Diamonds' uniforms that year, but since taking it on (at San Diego's behest) we knew the name meant something beyond a label worn by a new roster each successive spring. "Diamonds—7 P.M.—VFW" on the calendar for some snowy night in January meant us. *Waterloo Diamonds*, as Richard Panek wrote it, gives well more than half its space to particulars of the club's off-field operation, and giving those particulars a meaningful center is his characterization of Mildred Boyenga.

We see Mildred at city council meetings, frustrated with the politicians' unwillingness to sympathize with baseball's plight or even try to understand. We see her at board meetings, regretting how things aren't the way they used to be. But to Richard's credit, we also see her in private moments, times she shared with him alone, driving around the city to nooks and crannies a visitor would never find, even out into the countryside to the tiny town where Mildred grew up and where her ninety-year-old mother still lived.

This latter style of passage is what distinguishes Richard's book from sportswriting in particular and from nonfiction narrative in general. He himself is nowhere in the book, but because of his closeness to Mildred, his chief character, he is everywhere. Far beyond the flashier techniques of the New Journalism, Richard's method emulates the best features of creative work. What Mildred told him, he has her think. What they did together gets recounted as her private memories.

At one point in the midst of his research, before his theme coalesced and the club's fortunes took their last, decisive turn toward ruin, Mildred had shown him another graveyard in town. For such a venture, the day must have been a happy one, the weather clear and everything fresh. In *Waterloo Diamonds*, however, Richard saves this scene for the end—after all alternatives have failed, the club has been sold, and the atmosphere is as depressing as can be.

Here, as board members try to enliven the gloom by singing "Happy Birthday" to this ever-aging woman, Richard shows her pausing to think about possible regrets and then banishing them from her mind. But instead of returning attention to her friends, she stays with her memories for a bit longer, just enough for Richard to end his book. As the ball club dies before her, she travels back to that brighter day more than a year before, when on the nicest afternoon of early autumn she'd noticed a lovely, quiet corner of the cemetery where a perfect site lay yet unclaimed. Here she'd paused, felt the warmth of the earth, and looked through the branches of a shade tree to the nurturing sky, feeling more at peace than she had for years.

As the meeting continues around her, Mildred stays in her world of gentle rest. In her memories, she commits to purchasing the plot, then leaves. As Richard puts it in his own last words, "Mildred Boyenga brushed the dirt from her hands and, for now, walked away from her grave." Writing her own last chapter of baseball history, as Richard Panek's character, she makes herself immortal.

JERRY KLINKOWITZ has been a minor league baseball owner, operator, and consultant for over twenty years. During the off-season, he teaches at the University of Northern Iowa. He has written over thirty books on sports, literature, music, art, philosophy, military history, and other aspects of contemporary life and culture. His fiction includes *Basepaths* and *Short Season*.